SPiN

Workbook

3

Catherine Milton

NATIONAL
GEOGRAPHIC
LEARNING

CENGAGE
Learning·

Australia • Brazil • Japan • Korea • Mexico • Singapore • Spain • United Kingdom • United States

Spin 3 Workbook
Catherine Milton

Publisher: Gavin McLean

Director of Content Development: Sarah Bideleux

Managing Editor: Angela Cussons

Art Director: Natasa Arsenidou

Cover Designer: Natasa Arsenidou

Text Designer / Compositor: Sofia Fourtouni

National Geographic Liaison: Leila Hishmeh

Acknowledgements

Editorial management by Process ELT /
Georgia Zographou

Production project management by
Sofia Fourtouni

For permission to use material from this text or product,
submit all requests online at **www.cengage.com/permissions**

Further permissions questions can be emailed to
permissionrequest@cengage.com

ISBN: 978-1-4080-6107-7

National Geographic Learning
Cheriton House
North Way
Andover
Hampshire
SP10 5BE
United Kingdom

Cengage Learning is a leading provider of customized learning solutions with office locations around the globe, including Singapore, the United Kingdom, Australia, Mexico, Brazil and Japan. Locate your local office at:
international.cengage.com/region

Cengage Learning products are represented in Canada by
Nelson Education, Ltd.

Visit National Geographic Learning online at **ngl.cengage.com**

Visit our corporate website at **www.cengage.com**

Photo credits

Cover image: Kani Polat/NGIC. Hot air balloons, Cappadocia.

3-73 (all) Shutterstock, **74** Pierre Verdy/AFP/Getty Images/NGIC, **76-88** (all) Shutterstock

NGIC = National Geographic Image Collection

Printed in the United Kingdom by Ashford Colour Press Ltd.

Print Number: 11   Print Year: 2024

Contents

Introduction

1 Put the words in the correct order to make sentences.

1 horrible / Jenny / to her sister / never / is
   Jenny is never horrible to her sister.

2 is / drink / hot / to / this tea / too
   _____

3 to see / this film / are / the children / enough / old / not
   _____

4 ? / watch TV / you / in the morning / often / do
   _____

5 ? / in this room / enough / is / warm / it
   _____

6 usually / on Fridays / go home / we / early
   _____

2 Complete the sentences with these words.

   hers   his   mine   ours   theirs   yours

1 This book is _____ _mine_ _____ I bought it yesterday.
2 'I can't find my pink shirt. Can I borrow _____?' 'Sure.'
3 'Which CDs belong to Mike and Tim?' 'These ones are _____.'
4 'Is that Mary's laptop?' 'Yes, it's _____.'
5 This house is _____ We live next to the Martins.
6 The rucksack isn't George's. _____ is the black one.

3 Look at the pictures and write T (true) or F (false).

1	2	3
4	5	

1 Neither of the boys are bored.   F
2 There isn't much cheese on the plate. ☐
3 She is going to wear either the pink
   or the blue dress. ☐

4 Both boys are playing video games.   ☐
5 There are only a few strawberries
   in the bowl.   ☐

4 Circle the correct words.

Amy: I'm really hungry. Has Mum made **(1)** anything / anywhere for lunch?

Tim: No, she had to go **(2)** somewhere / something with Grandma. Shall we make a pizza?

Amy: Sure! Have we got **(3)** everything / everybody we need?
Is there **(4)** some / any cheese in the fridge?

Tim: Well, there's **(5)** a few / a little, but I don't think there's enough for a pizza. There are **(6)** a few / a little olives and there's **(7)** some / any ham.

Amy: Yuck. I hate olives. What about bacon? I love bacon on a pizza.

Tim: Sorry, there's **(8)** a little / no bacon. I ate it all for breakfast.

Amy: I know … where's the phone?

Tim: Why? What are you going to do?

Amy: Hello. Dino's Pizzas? I want to order a big pizza with bacon, cheese and peppers, please!

5 Complete the sentences with question tags.

1 The boys played football yesterday, ___didn't they___?
2 She's very pretty, _____?
3 You don't know Alex, _____?
4 Carla has left, _____?
5 Harry lives near here, _____?
6 Mum didn't give you a message, _____?

6 Complete the sentences with adverbs of manner.

1 You've done very ___well___ (good) this term, James.
2 Children, I want you to play _____ (nice) together.
3 The cat climbed _____ (high) up into the tree and wouldn't come down.
4 I think Simon will _____ (easy) pass the exam.
5 Don't drive so _____ (fast)! It's dangerous!
6 Jake always arrives _____ (late) for class.
7 Please wash the vase _____ (careful).
8 Come here _____ (quick)! There's a snake in the garden!

Lesson 1

Vocabulary

1 **Complete the sentences with these words.**

| magnificent | mushrooms | nomads | starving | strange | temple |

1 There was an old stone _____temple_____ outside the village.

2 I am _____! Can we have lunch now?

3 _____ are groups of people who move from place to place.

4 That's _____. I put my bag in the Jeep, but I can't find it now.

5 Be careful! Some _____ aren't safe to eat.

6 We visited the Rocky Mountains last summer. They were truly _____.

2 **Match.**

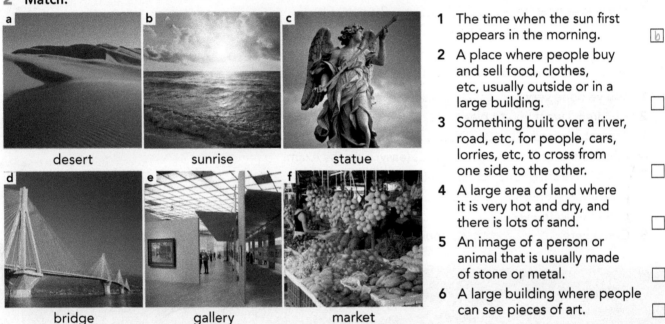

desert   sunrise   statue

bridge   gallery   market

1 The time when the sun first appears in the morning. `b`

2 A place where people buy and sell food, clothes, etc, usually outside or in a large building. ☐

3 Something built over a river, road, etc, for people, cars, lorries, etc, to cross from one side to the other. ☐

4 A large area of land where it is very hot and dry, and there is lots of sand. ☐

5 An image of a person or animal that is usually made of stone or metal. ☐

6 A large building where people can see pieces of art. ☐

3 **Circle the correct answers.**

1 fox
   a a wild animal with a thick tail
   b a plant that you can eat

2 barbecue
   a a meal made when food is cooked over a fire and eaten outdoors
   b an exotic meal cooked and eaten in a restaurant

3 guide
   a someone who manages a hotel
   b someone who takes tourists to a place and shows them around

4 landmark
   a a piece of art in a museum
   b something you can see from far away that helps you know where you are

5 shape
   a the form that something has
   b the size of something

Grammar

4 Complete the sentences with the Present Simple or the Present Continuous of these verbs.

book   leave   not answer   open   read   send   _speak_   walk

1 50% of the people who live in Montreal, Canada, _____ _speak_ _____ French.
2 Dad's online at the moment. He _____ our plane tickets to Egypt.
3 In this photo, we _____ in the White Desert.
4 The London Eye _____ at 10 am every day.
5 My dad always _____ a book when he travels by train.
6 _____ your sister _____ for Scotland this Wednesday?
7 She sometimes _____ me a card on my birthday.
8 He _____ his phone. Maybe he's out.

5 Write questions and short answers with the Present Simple or the Present Continuous.

1 they / stay near London ✓
   Are they staying near London?
   Yes, they are.

2 your friends / usually / enjoy travelling ✓
   _____
   _____

3 the tourists / visit the Great Temple tomorrow ✗
   _____
   _____

4 you / rent Jeeps in this shop ✓
   _____
   _____

5 Kristie / have lunch at the moment ✗
   _____
   _____

6 Complete the dialogue with the Present Simple or the Present Continuous of the verbs in brackets.

Bridget: (1) __Do you always come__ (you/always/come) to Ireland on holiday?

Damian: Yes, we (2) _____ (love) it here.

Bridget: (3) _____ (you/stay) at the campsite this week?

Damian: Yes, we are. Then next week we (4) _____ (drive) to Donegal Town.

Bridget: Donegal Town? (5) _____ (they/speak) Gaelic in Donegal?

Damian: Yes, but they (6) _____ (speak) English too. We (7) _____ (visit) the Old Castle on Wednesday and we (8) _____ (go) surfing at Rossnowlagh, a seaside beach resort, on Thursday.

Bridget: I hope you have a good time there. Enjoy yourselves!

Vocabulary

1 Complete the sentences with these words.

> away   back   down   in   in   off

1 I felt very dizzy when the plane took ___*off*___.
2 Are you excited about going _____ for the weekend?
3 Let's get _____ your Jeep and go for a drive in the desert.
4 We can't use the lift – it's broken _____.
5 My dad is in Portugal – he's coming _____ this Friday.
6 The first thing you do when you arrive at the airport is check _____.

2 Choose the correct answers.

1 Look at that view! It's ___!
  a frozen
  ⓑ spectacular
  c muddy

2 We're visiting the ancient Roman ___ today. Do you want to join us?
  a minerals
  b paths
  c ruins

3 Is the water in the river very ___?
  a deep
  b steep
  c wide

4 Slow down! This road is very ___!
  a narrow
  b flat
  c shallow

5 What time are your parents setting ___ in the morning?
  a across
  b about
  c off

3 Complete the dialogues with these words.

> damage   flow   form   pool   spring   terraces

1 A: It's hot. Let's go for a swim in the hotel ___*pool*___.
  B: Great idea!

2 A: How did the caves _____?
  B: I'm not sure, but it happened millions of years ago.

3 A: What are those things that look like steps on the side of the hill?
  B: They are _____. Farmers use them to grow vegetables.

4 A: Where does the hot water come from?
  B: It comes from a _____ 300 metres under the ground.

5 A: Does the river _____ into the sea?
  B: No, into the lake.

6 A: What caused the _____ to the castle?
  B: I think there was an earthquake here many years ago.

Grammar

4 **Complete the sentences with the Present Simple or the Present Continuous of these verbs.**

belong   drive   know   not understand   see   ~~smell~~   think

1 Those wild flowers near the path _____ smell _____ wonderful.
2 They _____ to Scotland because plane tickets are too expensive.
3 I _____ these instructions. Can you help me?
4 Who _____ this camera _____ to?
5 I can't join you – I _____ Kelly tonight.
6 She _____ of becoming an actress, but she's not sure yet.
7 I haven't got a map. _____ you _____ where the waterfall is?

5 **Complete the email with the Present Simple or the Present Continuous of the verbs in brackets.**

⚫⚫⚫   **Email**

📝 New   📩 Reply   📧 Forward   🖨 Print   🗑 Delete   📬 Send & Receive

Hi Stephanie,

Guess what? I **(1)** _____ am staying _____ (stay) in a hotel in Houston, Texas, for the summer! It **(2)** _____ (belong) to my Uncle Will. It's fantastic! Uncle Will **(3)** _____ (own) two small hotels in the city but this one is my favourite. I've got my own room and I **(4)** _____ (love) it! You can see me and Uncle Will outside the hotel in the photo I **(5)** _____ (send) you with this email. He **(6)** _____ (take) me to Splash Town, a water park in Houston, tomorrow. I can't wait! You **(7)** _____ (know) how much I like water slides! **(8)** _____ (you/have) a good time in Greece?
Send me an email and tell me all about it.

Love from Nancy

---

6 **Circle the correct words.**

1 This mountain path looks dangerous. Are you seeing / (Do you see) what I mean?
2 I am thinking / think this place is spectacular!
3 I am seeing / see my boss today at nine o'clock.
4 I am not thinking / don't think you can go into the temple.
5 I am thinking / think of going swimming in a hot water spring.
6 'They didn't pay for the tickets. They got them for free.' 'Oh I am seeing / see.'

Vocabulary

1 Write the missing letters.

1 People who travel or visit a place for fun.   t o u r i s t s
2 The place that someone is going to.   d _ _ _ _ _ _ _ _ _ _
3 Someone who is between 13 and 19 years old.   t _ _ _ _ _ _ _
4 A large area of water with land all around it.   l _ _ _
5 A system of tracks on which trains run.   r _ _ _ _ _ _
6 An area of land that is wet most of the time.   w _ _ _ _ _ _
7 The way from one place to another.   r _ _ _ _

Grammar

2 Complete the sentences with when, where, which, who or whose and these phrases.

> goes surfing   I spent last summer   is called the Toy Train   sister visited New Zealand
> they made the first *Lord of the Rings* film

1 A surfer is a person _who goes surfing_____.
2 2000 is the year _____.
3 A special train, _____, goes to the town of Darjeeling.
4 Mary, _____, wants to travel there too.
5 Lake Kerkini, _____, is a very important wetland.

Express yourself!

3 Match.

1 When's your mum's birthday?   a Once a year.
2 What are you doing at the moment?   b It's at three o'clock.
3 How often do you go on holiday?   c No, never. I'm always early.
4 Are you ever late for school?   d On 2nd September.
5 What time is your English lesson?   e No, I usually take the bus.
6 Do you walk to school?   f I'm reading a book about the Himalayas.

Writing

4 Complete the description of Katherine's home town with these words and phrases.

it is   there are   there is   they are   when   where   ~~which~~   who

I live in a market town **(1)** _____which_____ is called Alford. **(2)** _____ in Lincolnshire in the east of England. The best time to visit Alford is in the summer, **(3)** _____ the weather is warm and sunny.

Near Alford **(4)** _____ an impressive old castle called Bolingbroke Castle **(5)** _____ visitors can learn about life in the past and watch Shakespeare plays. The tourists **(6)** _____ visit the castle can see ruins of the old stone walls and towers.

You can also go to the beach in Mablethorpe, or visit the gardens in Claythorpe. **(7)** _____ full of beautiful flowers in the summer and **(8)** _____ over 500 birds flying around you! It's truly a little piece of paradise!

Remember!

We use There is/are to talk about something that exists or happens that we mention for the first time.

We use It is and They are to refer to something that has already been mentioned or is being talked about now.

There is a bridge across the river. It is made of wood.
There are four tourists in the souvenir shop. They are from New Zealand.

5 Write a description of your village or town. Include relative clauses, There is, There are, It is and They are. Use this plan to help you.

Paragraph 1
Give the name of your village or town and say where it is situated.

Paragraph 2
Talk about what you can see and do there.

Paragraph 3
Talk about other activities or places of interest.

2 Lesson 1

Vocabulary

1 Find six science-related words. Then use these words to complete the sentences.

A	R	F	P	G	A	L	A	X	Y	M	P
S	W	G	R	F	B	B	L	F	F	E	E
T	L	K	O	Z	Q	G	P	W	R	A	P
R	M	H	J	L	G	R	X	O	J	P	Y
O	B	S	E	R	V	A	T	O	R	Y	C
N	I	D	C	D	X	M	S	M	B	S	D
O	K	D	T	E	L	E	S	C	O	P	E
M	J	L	O	F	W	N	M	A	C	U	T
E	N	P	R	O	C	K	E	T	O	B	R
R	E	I	K	W	P	M	A	B	M	I	Q

1 The large group of stars which our sun and its planets belong to is called a(n) _____galaxy_____.
2 If you want to see the mountains on the moon, you need a bigger _____.
3 Kristie visited the London Planetarium in the _____ in Greenwich Park.
4 When will the _____ land on the moon?
5 The famous _____, Nicolaus Copernicus, was the first one who said that the Earth moves round the sun.
6 We can use the _____ and watch the film on that wall.

2 Write the missing letters.

1 This means very big.
m _a_ _s_ _s_ _i_ _v_ _e_
2 The area beyond the Earth where the stars and planets are.
s _ _ _ _
3 The Earth is one.
p _ _ _ _ _ _
4 A picture of an object on the screen of a TV or computer.
i _ _ _ _ _
5 A place where you can see moving images of the sky at night.
p _ _ _ _ _ _ _ _ _ _ _

3 Circle the correct words.

1 The London Planetarium has got one of the largest projectors / images in Europe.
2 'How big is your TV dome / screen?' 'It's 18 inches.'
3 This laptop is tiny / enormous – it can fit into your pocket.
4 She was very angry when she found out / about the truth.
5 Our space / galaxy has got between 200 and 400 billion stars.
6 He shouted at me in front of everybody – it was so embarrassing / enormous.

Grammar

4 **Choose the correct answers.**

1 They ___ asleep while they were watching the documentary.
  a were falling
  b fall
  c fell

2 We were looking at the images on the screen and the teacher ___ to us.
  a talked
  b was talking
  c talks

3 ___ your science homework at seven o'clock last night?
  a You did
  b Did you
  c Were you doing

4 I ___ to the cinema yesterday because I wasn't feeling well.
  a didn't go
  b wasn't going
  c not going

5 His dad was checking his emails while his mum ___ a magazine.
  a is reading
  b read
  c was reading

6 ___ a show at the Planetarium when you phoned them?
  a They were watching
  b Did they watch
  c Were they watching

5 **Complete the sentences with the Past Simple or the Past Continuous of the verbs in brackets.**

Apollo 11

- Apollo 11's journey to the moon in 1969 **(1)** ___took___ (take) three and a half days.

- Neil Armstrong first **(2)** _____ (walk) on the moon on 21st July 1969, and half a billion people were watching him on televisions across the world.

- When pilot Buzz Aldrin **(3)** _____ (step) out of the spaceship to join Armstrong, he had to make sure not to lock the door because there was no handle on the outside.

- While Armstrong **(4)** _____ (walk) on the moon, he received a call from the American President, Richard Nixon.

- Armstrong's first moonwalk **(5)** _____ (last) two and a half hours. While Armstrong and Aldrin **(6)** _____ (get) ready to come back to Earth, one of the engines had a problem and Aldrin fixed it using a pen!

- Armstrong and Aldrin spent 22 hours on the moon.

6 **Look at the pictures of these two people that were taken three years ago. Make sentences with used to.**

Lisa

Stephen

1 Lisa / go to work / by bike
  Lisa used to go to work by bike.

2 Lisa / wear / a helmet
  _____

3 Lisa / have / long hair
  _____

4 Stephen / work / on a farm
  _____

5 Stephen / have / a mobile phone
  _____

6 Stephen / wear / glasses
  _____

Vocabulary

1 Complete the crossword puzzle.

Across

1 How can I _____connect_____ this camera to my laptop?

3 We're making a _____ of a rocket. Do you want to help?

5 The film is about a man that lives in a _____ world, not the real world.

7 We can't use any of our office computers today – the whole _____ has stopped working.

Down

2 His dad works in a _____ that designs cars.

4 They can _____ 100 computers per hour.

6 If you want to start the DVD recorder, _____ the green button.

2 Circle the correct words.

1 We do / make all the experiments in the science lab.

2 Oh dear! I've done / made two mistakes in my maths test.

3 Have you had time to do / make your French homework?

4 Ssh! Don't do / make a sound or the birds will fly away.

5 We must do / make a decision about which printer to buy.

6 They have done / made some research into forms of life on the planet Mars.

7 He's not very good at science, but he's doing / making an effort to improve.

8 Mum, can you do / make me a favour, please?

3 Complete the dialogues with these phrasal verbs.

carry out   deal with   find out   point out   search for

1 A: If you have a problem, how do you _____deal with_____ it?
  B: I talk about it with my sister or my best friend.

2 A: Do you know if the concert is this Friday?
  B: I don't know, but I'll _____.

3 A: I need information about the Hubble Telescope.
  B: I'll help you _____ it.

4 A: We can go on a rock-climbing holiday!
  B: I think I should _____ how dangerous that is!

5 A: Do we know if there is another planet like Earth?
  B: No, we need to _____ more research.

14

Grammar

4 Complete the sentences with the Past Simple or the Present Perfect Simple of the verbs in brackets.

1 I _____watched_____ (watch) an amazing documentary about a new planet last night.
2 Kelly _____ (go) out. She'll be back later.
3 _____ (you/have) enough money to buy the tickets?
4 How many astronauts _____ (walk) on the moon since 1969?
5 He _____ (work) in a car company from 2009 to 2011.
6 _____ you _____ (ever/hear) of Laika, the first dog that travelled into space?
7 How long _____ (he/know) Jennifer?
8 She _____ (not take) the bus to London this morning. She went by train.

5 Circle the correct words.

Bright Inventions

Correction fluid

American typist Bette Graham **(1)** invented / has invented the correction fluid in the early 1950s. She was working as a secretary in a bank in Texas and she **(2)** corrected / has corrected her typing mistakes using white paint. She called it *Mistake Out* and started her own company in 1956. Since then, correction fluid and correction pens **(3)** made / have made life easier for thousands of people around the world.

Rolling luggage

Moving around the airport became less difficult when pilot Robert Plath **(4)** took / has taken a suitcase and added wheels. Pilots working for the same company asked him to do the same with their suitcases. Robert **(5)** started / has started his own company selling wheeled luggage in 1992. His company **(6)** was / has been very successful for the last 20 years because most travellers prefer buying wheeled luggage to non-wheeled luggage.

6 Complete the sentences with these words.

ago   already   ever   for   last night   never   since   yet

1 I've _____already_____ read that book about space travel. It was great.
2 The rocket left the Earth two months _____.
3 Tom has _____ been to the Science Museum and he really wants to go.
4 She has worked in this company _____ March 2009.
5 Her dad has been an astronomer _____ twelve years.
6 I haven't read all my emails _____.
7 Have you _____ played a virtual reality game?
8 A strange thing happened to me _____.

15

Vocabulary

1 Complete the sentences with these words.

discovery   gadget   invention   method   solar

1 Is the dishwasher or the microwave oven a more useful ___invention___?
2 What is the biggest planet in our _____ system?
3 Smartphones are a very popular _____.
4 Astronomers have made an important _____ about our galaxy.
5 Which scientific _____ is used to study climate change?

Express yourself!

2 Match.

1 He spoke so	a a small screen.
2 I got such	b that she went straight to bed.
3 The telephone is such	c dangerous.
4 She was so tired	d a useful invention.
5 Your laptop has got such	e quickly that I didn't understand him.
6 That cliff looks so	f bad marks for my history test.

Speaking

3 Work with a partner to make sentences. Use these prompts to talk about the people. Use so and such.

My mum
a good listener
kind
beautiful

My best friend
clever
a good student
funny

Justin Bieber
good-looking
great songs
famous

Writing

4 **Read the email below and put the paragraphs in the correct order.**

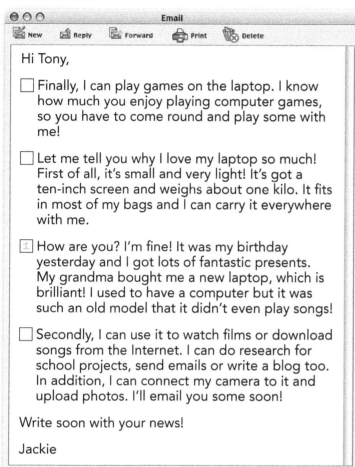

○○○   **Email**

📧 New   📧 Reply   📧 Forward   🖨 Print   🗑 Delete

Hi Tony,

☐ Finally, I can play games on the laptop. I know how much you enjoy playing computer games, so you have to come round and play some with me!

☐ Let me tell you why I love my laptop so much! First of all, it's small and very light! It's got a ten-inch screen and weighs about one kilo. It fits in most of my bags and I can carry it everywhere with me.

☐1 How are you? I'm fine! It was my birthday yesterday and I got lots of fantastic presents. My grandma bought me a new laptop, which is brilliant! I used to have a computer but it was such an old model that it didn't even play songs!

☐ Secondly, I can use it to watch films or download songs from the Internet. I can do research for school projects, send emails or write a blog too. In addition, I can connect my camera to it and upload photos. I'll email you some soon!

Write soon with your news!

Jackie

Remember!

We can use these words and phrases to put ideas in order in a letter or email.
Firstly/First of all/To start with
Secondly/In addition
Finally
We use *also* and *too* to add new points.
I can use my laptop to watch videos.
I can use it to listen to music too.
I can use my laptop to watch videos.
I can also use it to listen to music.

5 **Write an email to a friend about a new mobile phone. Include some words from the Remember! box. Use this plan to help you.**

Begin like this:
Hi _____ (your friend's name),

Paragraph 1
Say hello. Tell your friend why somebody gave you a new mobile phone.

Paragraph 2
Talk about the colour/shape/size of your mobile phone and say why you like it.

Paragraph 3
Talk about the best/most exciting things about your mobile phone.

Paragraph 4
Talk about what you can use your mobile phone for.

Finish like this:
Write soon with your news!
_____ (your name)

Reading

1 Read the text about the Iguazu Falls.

The spectacular Iguazu Falls, on the border between Brazil and Argentina in South America, are one of the New Seven Wonders of Nature. The Falls get their name from two words: *y*, which means 'water', and *uasu*, which means 'big'. The Iguazu Falls aren't just big, however, they are massive!

Small islands in the Iguazu River divide the Falls into many smaller waterfalls. These waterfalls can be from 60 metres high to 82 metres high. The number of the waterfalls may also change – sometimes there are as few as 150 waterfalls and sometimes there are as many as 300. The number depends on how much water there is in the river.

Today, people travel long distances to visit the Iguazu Falls. The Argentinean side has wider views of the Falls and you can go on a boat trip and get really close to them. However, on the Brazilian side there are special paths for tourists to walk on, and you can go on a helicopter ride to see the Falls from the air! Imagine that view!

2 Write R (Right), W (Wrong) or DS (Doesn't say).

1 The Iguazu Falls are in Brazil. `W`
2 There are seven New Wonders of Nature. ☐
3 The Falls are huge. ☐
4 The biggest waterfall is 80 metres high. ☐
5 There are more waterfalls in the summer. ☐
6 There are wider views of the Falls in Brazil. ☐

Vocabulary

3 Choose the correct answers.

1 How ___ is the water in this river?
  (a) deep
  b steep
  c narrow

2 Don't ___ a sound! I think there is something in our tent!
  a have
  b make
  c do

3 Does it often rain in the ___?
  a terrace
  b landmark
  c desert

4 Is this the art ___ where we can see da Vinci's famous paintings?
  a gallery
  b temple
  c bridge

5 We must follow the ___ along the river to the village.
  a statue
  b spring
  c path

6 What time does Stella's plane ___?
  a take off
  b check in
  c go away

7 Have you ever played a ___ reality game?
  a massive
  b tiny
  c virtual

8 Was Neil Armstrong the first man to walk on the ___?
  a galaxy
  b moon
  c star

9 I think this is the most ___ view I've ever seen!
  a shallow
  b spectacular
  c sandy

10 They were doing experiments to ___ how old the ruins were.
  a find out
  b deal with
  c carry out

11 A(n) ___ is a special building from which scientists can watch the moon, stars, weather, etc.
  a dome
  b projector
  c observatory

12 That company used to ___ cars but it's closed now.
  a press
  b produce
  c land

Grammar

4 Choose the correct answers.

1 We ___ to London tomorrow.
  a have driven
  (b) are driving
  c were driving

2 ___ visiting famous landmarks when you're on holiday?
  a Are you enjoying
  b Do you enjoy
  c Were you enjoying

3 We ___ a barbecue when it started to rain.
  a were having
  b had
  c have had

4 These mushrooms ___ awful!
  a taste
  b are tasting
  c were tasting

5 How long ___ this laptop?
  a you've had
  b did you have
  c have you had

6 The boy ___ father designs virtual reality games lives next door.
  a which
  b whose
  c who's

7 ___ the planetarium next week?
  a Is your class visiting
  b Does your class visit
  c Did your class visit

8 You can't go in! The doctor ___ someone at the moment.
  a sees
  b is seeing
  c has seen

9 ___ that book about the Sahara yet?
  a Did you finish
  b Have you finished
  c Were you finishing

10 Jim's not here – he's ___ to the post office.
  a gone
  b went
  c left

11 As we ___ in the woods, we saw a fox.
  a were walking
  b walked
  c have walked

12 We were looking for the hot springs when we ___ our way.
  a have lost
  b were losing
  c lost

Vocabulary

1 Complete the crossword.

Across

1 This is a flash of light in the sky during a bad storm.

4 This is the sound you often hear during a bad storm.

5 A storm and an earthquake are examples of this.

6 This can happen if there is heavy rain for a long time.

Down

2 This is when strong fast winds move over water.

3 This is a very frightening dream.

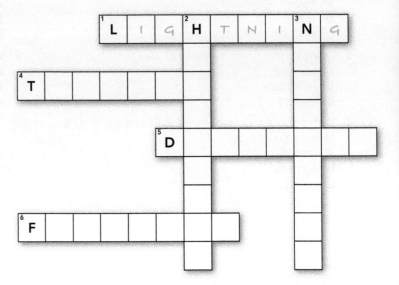

¹L	I	G	²H	T	N	I	³N	G

⁴T

⁵D

⁶F

2 The words in bold are in the wrong sentences. Write the correct words.

1 The **roofs** in our kitchen are falling off the walls.   *tiles*

2 The **storm** was started by a careless farmer.   _____

3 We heard a loud noise and then the house started to **cause**.   _____

4 People went up onto the **tiles** of their houses during the flood.   _____

5 Get into the house now! There is a bad **wildfire** coming!   _____

6 Did the hurricane **shake** this damage?   _____

3 Choose the correct answers.

1 shake
  a move slowly from side to side
  ⓑ move suddenly from side to side

2 volcano
  a a loud noise before a storm
  b a mountain with a large hole at the top

3 drought
  a a long period of heavy rain
  b a long period of dry weather

4 cause
  a make something bad happen
  b make the right decision

5 coast
  a the area where the land meets the sea
  b the area between two hills

Grammar

4 Choose the correct answers.

1 I ___ to this restaurant for years.
   a) have been coming
   b come
   c been coming

2 ___ has the ground been shaking?
   a What
   b How long
   c What time

3 ___ watching the news on TV? There was a tsunami in India.
   a You have been
   b Have you been
   c You haven't been

4 It ___ all day today.
   a snows
   b is snowing
   c has been snowing

5 She ___ hard lately.
   a not been working
   b hasn't been working
   c not working

6 We've been waiting for you ___ three o'clock.
   a since
   b for
   c all

5 Write questions and answers with the Present Perfect Continuous and the words in brackets.

1 how long / you work on / your science project (two days)
   How long have you been working on your science project?
   I've been working on my science project for two days.

2 Jennifer / feel / well / lately (no)
   _____
   _____

3 the floods / carry away / people's cars (yes)
   _____
   _____

4 how long / Paul / work / as an architect (March)
   _____
   _____

5 you / study / for your exams / all day (yes)
   _____
   _____

6 Complete the email with the Present Perfect Continuous of the verbs in brackets.

⦿⦿⦿   **Email**

New   Reply   Forward   Print   Delete   Send & Receive

Hi Jacob,

How are you? Sorry it took me so long to write back. I (1) _haven't been doing_ (not do) anything fun or exciting! There was a terrible storm last Saturday afternoon and electricity was cut off in the evening. I couldn't use my computer or do anything else.
It (2) _____ (rain) since then! Can you believe it? It hasn't stopped for a minute. It (3) _____ (drive) me mad! Mum got very frightened on the night of the storm and she (4) _____ (not sleep) well lately. Our fence got broken and tiles have come off the roof. Dad (5) _____ (work) all day trying to fix the damage.

I (6) _____ (stay) at my aunt's house for the last two days. Things are a bit better here. The house is warm and it's got electricity! I (7) _____ (use) my aunt's laptop to send emails to my friends. (8) _____ (you/watch) TV? Have you heard about the storm?

Write back soon!

Laura

Vocabulary

1 **Complete the dialogues with these words.**

> endangered   extinction   habitat   man-made   nocturnal   rainforests

1 **A:** What is the natural _____habitat_____ of tarsiers?
  B: They live in the forests on the islands of south-east Asia.

2 **A:** The population of orangutans is getting smaller.
  B: I know. We have to do something to protect them from _____.

3 **A:** Do bats sleep at night?
  B: No, they are _____ – they are active at night.

4 **A:** Did you know that this lake is _____?
  B: Really? I can't believe that people have created something so beautiful!

5 **A:** Why are _____ so important?
  B: Because they produce 28% of the world's oxygen.

6 **A:** Are sea turtles a(n) _____ animal?
  B: Yes, there are seven kinds of sea turtles and all of them are in danger of extinction.

2 **Find six animal-related words. Then use these words to complete the sentences.**

S	J	D	U	E	Z	G	J	M	G	W	Z
C	L	A	W	S	Y	V	P	K	U	R	R
A	R	Y	V	W	B	E	A	K	J	J	B
L	W	B	S	N	H	D	W	J	J	P	O
E	J	W	G	H	T	K	V	V	C	Y	O
S	S	N	D	N	G	Q	F	T	L	U	F
A	B	H	D	N	S	X	U	Z	H	S	C
A	P	E	C	Q	H	O	R	N	S	H	M
X	Q	T	L	P	G	Y	H	X	R	E	A
K	D	F	L	Q	L	B	T	F	U	U	O

1 That tiny bird has got a huge fish in its
  _____beak_____ and it's about to eat it!

2 Which dogs have got nice soft
  _____?

3 My cat has hurt her _____ and
  she can't walk.

4 African rhinoceroses have got two
  _____ but Indian rhinoceroses
  have got one.

5 Fish haven't got hair on their bodies –
  they've got _____.

6 Cats use their _____ to catch
  and hold their food.

3 **Complete the sentences with these words.**

> away   down   into   out   out   up

1 Don't throw ____away____ those old magazines. We can take them to the
  special recycling bins.

2 I can't print the invitations. We've run _____ of paper.

3 We're cleaning _____ the beach this Sunday. Why don't you join us?

4 How can we turn wind power _____ electricity?

5 Trees are often cut _____ and then sold to make furniture.

6 Mountain gorillas will die _____ if we don't protect them.

Grammar

4 **Complete the sentences with the Present Perfect Simple or the Present Perfect Continuous of the verbs in brackets.**

1 I _____have read_____ (read) this article about dinosaurs twice, but I still can't understand why they died out.

2 Tom _____ (not rest) all morning. He's been doing his science project.

3 _____ (you/see) the film *Ice Age*? It's very funny.

4 We _____ (just/finish) cleaning up the park. I'm very tired.

5 Karen _____ (not sleep) well since the earthquake.

6 George _____ (not phone) me for weeks.

7 We _____ (learn) about endangered animals at school all this week.

8 How many times _____ (you/be) to the Natural History Museum?

5 **Circle the correct words.**

1 Have you worked / Have you been working in the garden all day?

2 I have watched / have been watching this brilliant programme about tarsiers. Come and watch it with me!

3 Ollie has read / has been reading this book four times. He loves it!

4 I have been finding / have found a huge spider in the sitting room.

5 We haven't had / haven't been having anything to eat all day. We're starving!

6 Her hair is wet. She has swum / has been swimming in the pool.

6 **Choose the correct answers.**

1 They ___ three models of dinosaurs that look real. They are brilliant!
   a have made
   b make
   c have been making

2 What ___ lately?
   a you have been doing
   b have you been doing
   c have you done

3 Look! I ___ this amazing site about sea turtles on the Internet.
   a have found
   b have been finding
   c find

4 She ___ a fashion magazine all morning and she still hasn't finished it.
   a read
   b has been reading
   c has read

5 I ___ for information about animals in danger all morning.
   a have looked
   b looked
   c have been looking

6 ___ on this project for years! When will he finish it?
   a He has worked
   b Has he been working
   c He has been working

Vocabulary

1 Circle the correct words.

1 Can you help me plant the panels / (seeds) in the garden?
2 Remember to turn off / look after the lights when you leave the classroom.
3 I always have lunch in the canteen – school lunchtimes / lunches are very tasty!
4 We watered / picked some apples and made apple pie.
5 The air we breathe / grow is polluted.
6 Can you switch off / switch on your computer if you have finished? You're wasting energy.
7 They save / collect rainwater and water their plants with it.

Grammar

2 Complete the article with the correct comparative or superlative structure of the adjectives or adverbs in brackets.

Students have been having a very exciting year at Chelmsford School. At the beginning of the year, they decided to start a 'Go Green' project. Students had to find ways to use **(1)** _____less_____ (little) energy and recycle **(2)** _____ (much) rubbish. Ten-year-old Pam Stuart, one of the **(3)** _____ (young) students on the project, said, 'It was the **(4)** _____ (good) idea! The students in Class 2B worked the **(5)** _____ (hard) and collected glass bottles, batteries, cans, old magazines and newspapers.' The school had a competition and the winners were the students who cycled to school every day for a month. 'I did something great for the planet, and I feel **(6)** _____ (healthy) than ever before! Taking the bus is **(7)** _____ (slow) than riding your bike in a busy city,' said one of the winners. Looking after the environment is a lot **(8)** _____ (easy) than you think!

Express yourself!

3 Complete the sentences with it's worth or it isn't worth.

1 Don't go by car. The shop is just around the corner.
   _____It isn't worth going by car_____ because _____the shop is just around the corner_____.
2 Don't cook fish. Tom doesn't like it.
   _____ because _____.
3 You must go to the gallery. It's got some fantastic paintings.
   _____ because _____.
4 Don't wait. The next train leaves in five hours.
   _____ because _____.
5 Buy first-class tickets. The journey will be more comfortable.
   _____ because _____.

Writing

4 Read Julia's letter to a magazine about rubbish in her town and circle the correct words.

Dear Sir/Madam,

Last week there was an article in your magazine about rubbish and the environment. I **(1)** agree / disagree that we must find ways to deal with the huge rubbish problem in our town, and on this planet!

There are three beautiful parks in our town, but there are very few litter bins. That's why there's so much rubbish everywhere. It's terrible! Another problem is that you can only find recycling bins near the main square. People who want to recycle have to walk or drive there. In my **(2)** belief / opinion, we must put more litter bins in our parks and recycling bins in every neighbourhood.

I also think that we should have a 'clean-up day' every month. People can help clean up the parks and collect rubbish that can be recycled. It **(3)** is / isn't true that there's very little we can do to protect the environment.

If more people start caring about the environment, then I **(4)** agree / believe our town will become cleaner and people will enjoy it more.

Yours faithfully,

Julia Parker

Remember!

You can use these words and phrases to give your opinion about something when you are writing a formal email or letter.
I (really) think/believe …
In my opinion/view …
It is/isn't true that …
I agree/disagree that …

5 Write a letter to a local newspaper giving your opinion about how your school can do more to help the environment. Use this plan to help you.

Begin like this:
Dear Sir/Madam,,

Paragraph 1
Mention an article in the newspaper that you have read about how each person can help the environment. Say if you agree or disagree.

Paragraph 2
Explain what the problems are and talk about one thing students and/or teachers can do. Say how this could be done and what the advantages are.

Paragraph 3
Talk about another thing students and/or teachers can do. Say how this could be done and what the advantages are.

Paragraph 4
Say what you believe will happen if schools do more to help the environment.

Finish like this:
Yours faithfully,

_____ (your full name)

25

Vocabulary

1 Write the missing letters.

1 A secret plan by a group of people to do something bad.   p <u>l</u> <u>o</u> <u>t</u>
2 When you do what you tried or wanted to.   s _ _ _ _ _ _
3 A brave man who fights for his king.   k _ _ _ _ _ _
4 The power or energy you need to do something hard.   e _ _ _ _ _ _
5 Someone who makes good decisions and gives good advice.   w _ _ _
6 An old, well-known story, often about brave people.   l _ _ _ _ _

2 Write the opposites of these adjectives using dis-, im-, ir-, un- or -less. Then use the opposites to complete the sentences below.

a careful   _____careless_____
b kind   _____
c patient   _____
d honest   _____
e pleasant   _____
f responsible   _____

1 You've broken my MP3 player! You're so
   _____careless_____!
2 He tells lies and cheats – he's _____.
3 Yuck! What is that _____ smell coming from the kitchen?
4 It's very _____ of you to talk on your mobile phone while you are driving. You could have an accident!
5 It was very _____ of you not to invite your sister to your party.
6 Don't be so _____! We've only been waiting for five minutes.

3 Write G (for something good) or B (for something bad). Then match the definitions a–e with some of the adjectives 1–10.

1	brave	G	6	weak	☐
2	mean	☐	7	generous	☐
3	cheerful	☐	8	foolish	☐
4	strong	☐	9	cowardly	☐
5	wise	☐	10	miserable	☐

a This person is not at all brave.   9
b This person hates spending money.   ☐
c This person behaves in a way that shows he/she is happy.   ☐
d This person is not strong physically.   ☐
e This person is extremely unhappy.   ☐

Grammar

4 Complete the sentences with the Past Perfect Simple of the verbs in brackets.

1 Mum _____ *hadn't locked* _____ (not lock) the door before she went to work. She had forgotten.

2 _____ (you/just/wake up) when she called you?

3 Jenny _____ (never/be) to Scotland before. It was her first time.

4 By ten o'clock the children _____ (not go) to sleep. They were still watching TV.

5 _____ (Tom/already/have) dinner when Pam got home?

6 Arthur became king after he _____ (pull) the sword out of the stone.

5 Choose the correct answers.

1 By Monday morning I ___ my project on ancient Greek mythology.
   a have finished
   b finished
   c had finished

2 Peter had visited the Callanish Standing Stones ___ he went back to the USA.
   a by
   b before
   c after

3 ___ 15th June he had finished all his exams.
   a By
   b Until
   c Already

4 Katy ___ ancient Greek at school, so she knew all the Greek myths.
   a have studied
   b had studied
   c study

5 ___ shopping before they went to the museum?
   a They had gone
   b Had they gone
   c They hadn't gone

6 I ___ of King Arthur until I read that book about myths and legends.
   a didn't hear
   b never heard
   c had never heard

6 Complete the sentences with the Past Perfect Simple of these verbs.

eat	invite	live	not check	not sleep	start

1 _____ *Had* _____ Arthur _____ *lived* _____ with Sir Ector before he became king?

2 Ten people came to my party last Saturday, but I _____ twenty.

3 Mike was tired because he _____ well the night before.

4 She _____ all her emails when she turned off her laptop.

5 _____ the film _____ when you got to the cinema?

6 I had a stomach ache because I _____ too much pizza!

Lesson 2

Vocabulary

1 **Complete the crossword puzzle.**

Across

2 The Moai people _____probably_____ went to Easter Island by canoe.

3 Australia was a British _____ in the 18th century.

5 I am Greek but my _____ were Italian.

6 The statue was placed on a _____ in the main square.

8 The land was very _____ and it was difficult to walk long distances.

Down

1 They will _____ the children to the theatre by coach.

4 They built the stone heads to _____ their king.

7 When did Marco Polo _____ to Venice from China?

2 **Circle the correct words.**

1 I don't think Anne is capable in / of moving the sofa on her own.

2 You won! I am so proud of / in you!

3 The police believe that a farmer is responsible about / for the forest fire.

4 I've always been interested in / with archaeology.

5 Amelia wasn't worried about / for doing well in her exam.

6 This TV series is very popular from / with young people.

7 Do you think this film is suitable for / in a ten-year-old child?

8 John was jealous about / of his brother because he was the most popular boy at school.

3 **Complete the sentences with these words.**

chance home impression job reply surprise

1 I was asleep when he got _____home_____ last night.

2 When she walks into the house and we're all there, she will get a big _____!

3 I called Bob earlier, but I didn't get a(n) _____.

4 She got a part-time _____ as a waitress.

5 I'm not sure I like Steven. I get the _____ that he's dishonest.

6 If I ever get the _____, I will visit Easter Island.

Grammar

4 **Complete the sentences using the Past Simple or the Past Perfect Simple.**

1 Emily cried. She cut her finger.
Emily _____*cried*_____ because she _____*had cut*_____ her finger.

2 Danny ate a lot of chocolate cake. He was ill.
Danny _____ ill because he _____ a lot of chocolate cake.

3 Zoe finished her project. Then she went to the cinema.
Zoe _____ her project when she _____ to the cinema.

4 I read the book in May last year. I saw the film in August last year.
I _____ the film after I _____ the book.

5 Mum cooked dinner at seven o'clock. Dad returned home at eight o'clock.
By the time Dad _____ home, Mum _____ dinner.

5 **Circle the correct words.**

1 John had never tried / never tried Polynesian food before.
2 I had just got in the shower when the phone had rung / rang.
3 Grandad had put / put presents under the bed before the children woke up.
4 By the time the detective got to the house, the thief had run away / ran away.
5 Did you ever see / Had you ever seen a real albatross before you went to the zoo?
6 She was worried because her daughter didn't call / hadn't called all day.

6 **Complete the sentences with the Past Simple or the Past Perfect Simple of the verbs in brackets.**

1 The Vikings ___*had aleady discovered*___ (already/discover) North America five hundred years before
Christopher Columbus _____*sailed*_____ (sail) there in 1492.

2 By the time the explorer Jacques-Yves Cousteau _____ (die) in 1997, he
_____ (write) many books.

3 Norway's Roald Amundsen _____ (already/be) to the South Pole when Englishman
Captain Scott _____ (arrive) there in 1912.

4 Amelia Earhart _____ (travel) to many places before she
_____ (fly) across the Atlantic Ocean.

5 No human being _____ (walk) on the moon before Neil Armstrong
_____ (step) out of Apollo 11 in 1969.

Vocabulary

1 Circle the correct words.

1 One day, a stranger turned / (appeared) in front of King Midas.
2 When Midas touched the flowers, they turned / became to gold.
3 Midas got a shock / pain because his breakfast had become gold.
4 Midas shouted / touched with pain.
5 The Golden Touch had made / was supposed to make Midas happy, but it didn't.
6 Midas threw away / gave up the Golden Touch and became a happier man.

Express yourself!

2 Rewrite the sentences with the words given in brackets and any other words which are necessary.

1 Children, I wanted you to put your toys away. (supposed)
The children _____*were supposed to put*_____ their toys away.

2 Sarah wanted to read about King Arthur, but she couldn't find her book. (going)
Sarah _____ about King Arthur, but she couldn't find her book.

3 Gary forgot to take the rubbish out. (supposed)
Gary _____ the rubbish out.

4 We hadn't planned to tell him the truth, but he found out anyway. (going)
We _____ him the truth, but he found out anyway.

5 Jack's mother told him not to stay up late, but he didn't listen. (supposed)
Jack _____ but he didn't listen.

Speaking

3 Tell your partner about the things you were/weren't supposed to do and the things you were/weren't going to do.

I wasn't supposed to eat all the cake, but I did.

I was going to go to the cinema but I changed my mind.

Writing

4 Read the traditional story from Britain and circle the correct words.

(1) Suddenly / Once upon a time, there was a poor boy named Jack. Jack and his mother lived in a little house. They didn't have much money – all they had was a cow. **(2)** One day / Finally, the cow stopped giving milk and Jack's mother sent Jack to the market to sell it.

(3) Soon / As soon as Jack got to the market, an old man asked him to give him the cow. The old man didn't have any money but he gave Jack some magic beans. Jack took the magic beans and returned home. **(4)** After that / At first, Jack gave the beans to his mother. She was very angry with her son and she threw the beans out of the window.

(5) The next morning / Finally, a huge plant had grown in Jack's garden. He climbed the plant and saw an enormous palace – it was the home of a terrible giant. Jack got into the palace and found a place to hide. While the giant was sleeping, he took a chicken that produced golden eggs and left the palace. The giant saw Jack and ran after him!

While the giant was climbing down the plant, Jack cut the plant and the giant fell on the ground and died. **(6)** In the end / At the beginning, Jack and his mother didn't have to worry about money any more and lived happily ever after.

Remember!

You can use these words and phrases to tell a story.
Once upon a time, At the beginning
One day/morning/night
In the end, Finally
After a while, Suddenly, About an hour later, Then, After that, The next thing I knew, Soon

5 Write a traditional story from your country. Use the questions in the plan to help you.

Paragraph 1
Who is the main character?
Where did he/she live?

Paragraph 2
What happened first?
What happened after that?

Paragraph 3
What happened next? How did the story develop?

Paragraph 4
How did the story end?

Reading

1 Read the text about the Philippine Eagle.

The Philippine Eagle, also known as the Monkey-eating Eagle, only lives in the forests of the Philippines. It's the national bird of the Philippines and it was first discovered by John Whitehead, an English explorer, in 1896. Tribesmen told Whitehead that the eagles only ate monkeys and he called them 'monkey-eating eagles'. This was not true, however, because they also eat lemurs, snakes, lizards and birds.

The Philippine Eagle is one of the largest and most powerful birds in the world. It has long brown feathers, a dark face, yellow legs with strong claws and a blue beak. The mother and father eagle stay together for life. They both look after their babies and hunt for food to feed them.

The population of this species has become smaller mainly because people have been destroying its natural habitat. In 1969 a protection programme was started to help preserve it, but unfortunately, there are fewer than 500 eagles today. The Philippine Eagle has been on the list of endangered species since 2010 and there are now special protected areas for it. Let's hope we haven't run out of time and we can still save it!

2 Answer the questions.

1 Where do Monkey-eating Eagles live?
   In the forests of the Philippines.

2 What do the eagles eat?
   _____

3 What colour are the eagles' beaks?
   _____

4 Who takes care of the babies?
   _____

5 When did people start protecting the eagles?
   _____

6 How many eagles are there today?
   _____

Vocabulary

3 Choose the correct answers.

1 A ___ is a long period of dry weather.
  a tsunami
  b flood
  (c) drought

2 A(n) ___ is a large amount of water that covers an area that is usually dry.
  a wildfire
  b earthquake
  c flood

3 When I first met him, I got the ___ that he was dishonest.
  a chance
  b impression
  c reply

4 After the French had travelled to Canada, they set up a big ___ in Nova Scotia.
  a colony
  b effort
  c plot

5 This gadget has not been very popular ___ younger users.
  a with
  b in
  c for

6 The wildfire ___ a lot of damage to houses and forests.
  a shook
  b caused
  c destroyed

7 How many years ago did dinosaurs die ___?
  a down
  b up
  c out

8 He had been ___ and now the magic sword was gone.
  a careless
  b responsible
  c careful

9 Before my grandfather died, he had told me many things about my ___.
  a ancestors
  b islanders
  c knights

10 He was a weak, ___ man who ran away when he saw the enemy.
  a patient
  b cowardly
  c wise

11 It was one of the worst natural ___ in history – we are lucky to be alive.
  a habitats
  b disasters
  c extinctions

12 The Mediterranean monk seal is one of the most ___ species today. There were only 600 monk seals left in 2011.
  a endangered
  b man-made
  c nocturnal

Grammar

4 Choose the correct answers.

1 ___ has it been snowing?
  a For very long
  (b) How long
  c When

2 She hasn't been feeling very well ___.
  a recently
  b a long time
  c by then

3 He ___ the Callanish Standing Stones since 2007.
  a studies
  b is studying
  c has been studying

4 ___ the book about Arthur and his knights before you saw the film?
  a Had you read
  b Have you read
  c Have you been reading

5 How long ___ Chinese?
  a have you been learning
  b did you learn
  c do you learn

6 Maths is ___ school subject.
  a interesting than
  b the most interesting
  c most interesting

7 I can understand English ___ than Russian.
  a easiest
  b more easily
  c too easily

8 This has been ___ wildfire in twenty years.
  a the worst
  b worst
  c worse

9 Dad had taken us to a safe place ___ the time the hurricane started.
  a in
  b from
  c by

10 She ___ the old newspapers to the recycling centre.
  a has already taken
  b has already been taking
  c already takes

11 I ___ to the Island of Lewis before last year.
  a have never been
  b had never been
  c never went

12 We were tired. We ___ all day.
  a have been working
  b are working
  c had been working

Lesson 1

Vocabulary

1 **Complete the dialogues with these words.**

> course   employ   local   occupation   perfect   qualifications

1 **A:** They will _____*employ*_____ a new chef for the hotel restaurant.
   B: Do you think I should apply?

2 **A:** A journalist from the _____ newspaper wants to interview you!
   B: Why? I'm not famous.

3 **A:** I'm sure you will get the job because you've got a lot of experience.
   B: That's true! But I haven't got any _____.

4 **A:** What's your _____, Martin?
   B: I'm a biologist.

5 **A:** He's going to study economics in France.
   B: That's why he's doing a language _____ in French.

6 **A:** Do you like being a video game tester?
   B: Like it? It's the _____ job for me!

2 **Write the missing letters.**

1 The money you get every month when you work.   s _a_ _l_ _a_ _r_ _y_
2 A qualification you get when you finish university or college.   d __ __ __ __ __
3 You work for this person.   e __ __ __ __ __ __ __
4 When you ask for something like a job or a place at university.   a __ __ __ __ __
5 A job that you do for a long period of your life.   c __ __ __ __ __
6 An activity or piece of work you have to do.   t __ __ __

3 **Complete the sentences with the correct word.**

> journalism   journalist

1 I've decided I'm going to study ____*journalism*____ at university.

> attractive   attraction

2 Going to Paris for the weekend sounds like a very _____ idea.

> employer   employee

3 I'm an _____ at that restaurant. I've worked there since May.

> advert   advertising

4 Companies spend thousands of pounds on _____ every week.

> program   programmer

5 He's got a job as a computer _____ in an IT company.

> blog   blogger

6 My cousin has got the most amazing job – he's a video _____.

Grammar

4 Choose the correct answers.

1 I think I'll get the job.
   a It's my opinion that I'll get the job.
   b It's certain that I'll get the job.

2 I'll phone my employer.
   a I've just decided to phone her.
   b I'm not sure if I will call her.

3 Look! That man's going to fall!
   a You can see someone falling.
   b Someone is going to fall in a few moments.

4 Don't worry! We'll drive you home.
   a We have just decided to drive you home.
   b We are thinking about driving you home.

5 My sister is going to study art at university.
   a She is studying art at university now.
   b She is planning to study art at university.

5 Circle the correct words.

1 Adrian has booked plane tickets to Italy. He **is going to** / will fly to Rome on 1st May.
2 She doesn't have the right qualifications. I think she **isn't going to** / **won't** get the job.
3 Gary's trip is very dangerous. I hope he **is going to** / **will** be all right.
4 Rob **isn't going to** / **won't** sell his car. He told me last night.
5 Look at Jim! He **will** / **is going to** drop those glasses.
6 I hope we **aren't going to** / **won't** miss the beginning of the film.

6 Complete the dialogue with the Future Simple or be going to and the verbs in brackets.

Jake: Hi Ellie. You look very excited about something. **(1)** _Are you going to tell_ (you/tell) me your news, or do I have to guess?

Ellie: Hi Jake! You **(2)** _____ (not believe) this, but I **(3)** _____ (fly) to Sydney on 3rd December! I got a job working as a trainer on a cruise ship, and I'll be there for three months.

Jake: Wow! That is exciting! I'm sure that it **(4)** _____ (be) an amazing experience! What **(5)** _____ (you/do) with your pets?

Ellie: Well, I hope you **(6)** _____ (not mind) looking after them! I know you're very good with animals.

Jake: No problem! That's what friends are for!

5 Lesson 2

Vocabulary

1 **Complete the crossword puzzle.**

Across

1 There's a ___sculpture___ of a gigantic insect outside the art gallery.
5 He used thousands of toy _____ to make this castle.
6 Have you ever seen Katy Perry _____ in concert? She's fantastic!
7 The competition is the most important sports _____ of the year.

Down

2 I'm a lucky man. I had fantastic parents and a very happy _____.
3 By this time tomorrow, she will have finished painting my _____.
4 There's an _____ of Picasso's work at the museum.

```
[1]S [2]C  U  L [3]P  T  U  R [4]E
    C             P             E
    C             P          [5]B
    C             P
    C             P          [6]L
    C             P
    C             P
            [7]E              
```

2 **Match.**

1 fashion designer   a I build or fix houses.
2 builder   b I design clothes.
3 carpenter   c I fix baths and toilets.
4 journalist   d I write news reports for newspapers, TV or radio.
5 architect   e I design buildings.
6 plumber   f I create sculptures.
7 sculptor   g I make or fix wooden things.

3 **Complete the sentences with these words.**

~~down~~ down off on through

1 I hope I get the job, but I'm afraid they will turn me ___down___.
2 My brother wanted to be an artist but my mum put him _____.
3 Will the company be taking _____ any new employees this month?
4 We've got a lot to get _____ today, so let's start.
5 Can you put _____ your address and full name on this form, please?

Grammar

4 **Complete the sentences with the Future Continuous of these verbs.**

do   land   make   move   not study   write

1 The explorers _____ will be making _____ a long journey across the mountains.
2 _____ Debbie _____ into her new flat this time next week?
3 He _____ articles for the newspaper as he travels around South America.
4 _____ we _____ at Gatwick Airport in the next hour?
5 Next week the children _____ a project about 18th century sculptors.
6 I can join you. I _____ for my exams this weekend.

5 **Circle the correct words.**

1 Will we be having / We will be having chicken for lunch on Sunday?
2 During / At this time tomorrow we'll be sitting on the beach!
3 This time yesterday / tomorrow I'll be interviewing Paul Simon, the famous artist!
4 Don't call me at seven o'clock – I will be sleeping / am sleeping.
5 I'll be going to the supermarket now / later. Do you need anything?
6 What will Jack be doing / will Jack do at this time tomorrow?

6 **Look at the diary and complete the sentences with the Future Continuous.**

Diary	
Monday	Fly to Mali, West Africa
Tuesday	stay in Bamaco, capital of Mali, one day
Wednesday	visit Dogon village, see famous mud buildings
Thursday	buy food, get ready for the trip to Niger River
Friday	go on a river trip, put up our tents at the campsite
Saturday	relax at the campsite

1 On Monday, we _____ will be flying _____ to Mali in West Africa.
2 On Tuesday, we _____ in Bamaco, the capital of Mali, for one day.
3 On Wednesday, we _____ Dogon village to see the famous mud buildings.
4 On Thursday, we _____ food and we _____ ready for our trip to the Niger River.
5 On Friday, we _____ on a river trip and then we _____ our tents at the campsite.
6 On Saturday, we _____ at the campsite!

Vocabulary

1 Choose the correct answers.

1 creative
   a proud of what you have done
   (b) good at producing new ideas or things

2 ambition
   a when you want to succeed in something
   b when you have qualifications for a job

3 tour
   a a planned journey by musicians
   b a long and tiring journey

4 give up
   a start doing something
   b stop doing something

5 waste time
   a have very little free time
   b spend more time than is useful

6 action photography
   a taking photos of people or things that are moving fast
   b taking photos of famous athletes

Grammar

2 Rewrite the sentences. Use the Future Perfect Simple.

1 Jenny is finishing her article on advertising. It has to be ready on Monday morning.
   By Monday morning, Jenny _____will have finished_____ her article on advertising.

2 On 5th August, he will start working for the new company.
   By 6th August, he _____ working for the new company.

3 I will have ten driving lessons and then I will take my driving test.
   I _____ ten driving lessons by the time I take my driving test.

4 Our shop is closing in one hour. We won't sell all these T-shirts before we close.
   We _____ all these T-shirts before we close the shop.

5 The children will go to bed at eight o'clock. Their dad will come home at nine o'clock.
   The children _____ to bed by the time their dad comes home.

Express yourself!

3 Look at the pictures and complete the sentences with be about to and these verbs.

    do interview leave listen paint play

Mrs Hill _is about to interview_ the man.

Sheila _____ to her favourite song.

He _____ the housework.

The artist _____ a portrait.

The children _____ for school.

Jo and Ann _____ tennis.

Writing

4 **Read the article and choose the best topic sentence for each paragraph. Be careful – there is one sentence that you don't need.**

a Sherry loves swimming and hopes to become a famous swimmer one day.

b I'm sure that Sherry will succeed in making her dream come true.

c Sherry, who is my best friend, is one of the most energetic people I know.

d Sherry practises gymnastics twice a week.

Remember!

Each paragraph of your writing should begin with a topic sentence which tells us what the paragraph is about. The rest of the paragraph must follow logically from the topic sentence.

(1) _c_ She does gymnastics, plays baseball and she swims. She runs ten kilometres every evening and still has time to study for school and go out with her friends.

(2) ___ She's the best swimmer in our town and last year she took part in the local swimming competition. Although she is really funny and we always have a great time together, she is very serious about her ambitions. She belongs to the school team and trains at the pool for three hours every Saturday and Sunday.

(3) ___ She is going to start training with professional athletes next month, and I believe that she will amaze her coach with her abilities. I think that she will soon be in the national swimming team and will be winning gold medals for her country!

5 **Write an article about your best friend's ambitions and dreams. Make sure every paragraph starts with a topic sentence. Use this plan to help you.**

Paragraph 1
Describe your best friend and his/her abilities.

Paragraph 2
Say what his/her dream is and say how he/she is trying to make his/her dream come true.

Paragraph 3
Say if you think he/she will succeed.

Lesson 1

Vocabulary

1 **Complete the sentences with these words.**

apprentice   chemistry   genius   sculpting   submarine   weapon

1 Einstein was brilliant! He was a(n) _____genius_____ in both maths and science.
2 My sister works in a hairdresser's as a(n) _____.
3 _____ is my favourite school subject and I enjoy doing experiments in the lab.
4 How long can this _____ stay under water?
5 The young artist has studied drawing, painting and _____.
6 'Put down your _____ now,' shouted the police officer.

2 **Choose the correct answers.**

1 Andy, who studied ___, works for a big company.
  a biology
  b biologist

2 Paul is a talented young ___.
  a music
  b musician

3 Michelangelo was a famous ___ and painter.
  a sculptor
  b sculpture

4 What did you do in your ___ class today?
  a scientist
  b science

5 Alexander Graham Bell was a famous ___.
  a invention
  b inventor

6 There was a large ___ of his grandad on the wall.
  a painting
  b painter

3 **Look at the pictures and write the missing letters.**

1 e _n_ _g_ _i_ _n_ _e_ _e_ _r_

2 a _ _ _ _ _ _ _

3 m _ _ _ _ _ _ _

4 b _ _ _ _ _ _ _ _

5 p _ _ _ _ _ _ _ _

6 l _ _ _ _ _

Grammar

4 Circle the correct words.

1 Kate is interested in continuing / to continue her music career abroad.
2 My dad used to spend / spending all his free time gardening.
3 To study / Studying plants is an important part of her job as a biologist.
4 Do you enjoy to watch / watching science fiction films?
5 Tony is really good at painting / to paint portraits.
6 My friend has invited me to stay / staying at her house in Tuscany this summer!
7 I was sorry hearing / to hear that he had a car accident.

5 Look at the pictures and complete the sentences with the gerund or infinitive form of these verbs.

buy   cook   get up   paint   play   surf

Mum has just started _____cooking_____ dinner.

Billy learnt _____ when he was very young.

Amy and Jane are good at _____ the guitar.

Jacob always goes _____ in the summer.

Evelyn can afford _____ that dress.

I'm used to _____ early because I do it every day.

6 Complete the article with the gerund or the infinitive of the verbs in brackets.

Russian athlete Olga Korbut enjoyed **(1)** _____climbing_____ (climb) big trees and high walls at a very young age. She was the smallest student in her class, but she was the best at **(2)** _____ (run) and jumping. When she had her first gymnastics lesson, she fell in love with the sport. Olga used to spend all her time **(3)** _____ (train) and she got better and better. She joined the Russian national team at the age of fourteen and managed **(4)** _____ (win) three gold medals at the 1972 Olympic Games in Munich, Germany. Until then, very few people were interested in **(5)** _____ (watch) or reading about gymnastics. After the 1972 Olympics, thousands of girls wanted to be like Olga and decided **(6)** _____ (take up) gymnastics. She was really excited **(7)** _____ (have) so many fans, and in 1976 she won her fourth gold medal at the Olympic Games in Montreal, Canada.

Vocabulary

1 Choose the correct answers.

1 hospital
   a the place where people learn languages
   (b) the place where sick people are taken care of

2 crew
   a the people who work on a ship or plane
   b the members of a sports team

3 lifeboat
   a a boat that you can live in
   b a boat for people who are in danger at sea

4 fisherman
   a someone who swims very well
   b someone who catches fish as a job

5 wounded
   a injured or hurt
   b very tired

6 pour
   a fall from a high place
   b flow out of or into something

7 survivor
   a someone who continues to live after an accident, war or illness
   b someone who enjoys being in dangerous places

2 Complete the sentences with the correct form of give or take.

1 Our teacher always _____gives_____ us instructions before we do an experiment.

2 It _____ her a long time to get here because she had to walk.

3 Can you _____ care of your little sister while I'm out?

4 _____ me a call this afternoon if you're bored.

5 I think I've fixed your laptop. Come and _____ a look.

6 Joey _____ me an idea about where to look for a new job.

7 _____ my advice, Jim. You have to try harder if you want to succeed.

3 Circle the correct words.

1 My grandad became a soldier at / in the age of eighteen.

2 I found this painting in an antique shop quite for / by chance.

3 I'm sorry if I hurt your feelings – I didn't do it on / with purpose.

4 Sheila lost her job last May and has been away / out of work ever since.

5 Dennis was in / on his twenties when he first took part in the Olympic Games.

6 I've wanted to go to that gallery in / for ages! Thanks for inviting me!

Grammar

4 Write **S** if the sentences have the same meaning and **D** if they are different.

1

He went on to talk about endangered animals.
He went on talking about endangered animals.

2 ☐

He stopped to look for his keys.
He stopped looking for his keys.

3 ☐

I remembered signing the letter.
I remembered to sign the letter.

4 ☐

She continued to read the book.
She continued reading the book.

5 ☐

I like to watch adventure films.
I like watching adventure films.

6 ☐

She started making lunch.
She started to make lunch.

5 Choose the correct answers.

1 Try adding some salt to the soup.
(a) Why don't you add some salt to the soup?
b It's difficult to add salt to the soup.

2 Have you forgotten coming to my house before?
a Can't you remember that you've been to my house before?
b Did you forget to come to my house?

3 We need to stop to buy some water.
a We mustn't buy any more water.
b Let's buy some water.

4 She remembered to meet her aunt at the station.
a She remembered the time she met her aunt at the station.
b She didn't forget to go and meet her aunt at the station.

5 He forgot telling her about the exhibition.
a He told her about the exhibition but then forgot that he'd told her.
b He did not tell her about the exhibition.

6 She stopped crying and left for school.
a She didn't cry any more and left for school.
b She was still crying when she left for school.

6 Circle the correct words.

1 Can you please stop making / to make so much noise! I'm trying to study!
2 She was a musician and went on becoming / to become an actress.
3 I remember visiting / to visit Rome for the first time. It was an amazing trip!
4 Mum forgot to wake / waking me up this morning and I was late for school!
5 If your DVD recorder doesn't work, try to press / pressing the orange button.
6 I forgot calling / to call John and I'll do it now.

6 Lesson 3

Vocabulary

1 Complete the sentences with these words.

alive   complete   continent   crash   hits   inform   injured

1 How many runners managed to _____complete_____ the marathon race?
2 Australia is the smallest _____ and Asia is the largest.
3 I had an accident and I'm lucky to be _____.
4 They must _____ passengers about the changes in the timetable.
5 Was your brother badly _____ in the car accident?
6 This music site had more than a thousand _____ in its first week.
7 How did the helicopter _____ into the hill?

Speaking

2 Read the comments and talk to your partner about a birthday party. Use *too* and *enough*.

> Betty's birthday party was terrible! Her house was crowded and it was really noisy.

> There were hot dogs to eat, but they were cold.

> The birthday cake was small, so some of the guests didn't get any.

> The video games were really boring, so we didn't play any.

> Jimmy brought some of his CDs. It was supposed to be popular music, but it wasn't cool, so we didn't listen to it.

> The comedy that we were supposed to watch wasn't funny.

Express yourself!

3 Put the words in the correct order to make sentences.

1 competition / too / is / it / see / late / to / the
   It is too late to see the competition.
   _____

2 it / today / warm / sit / enough / isn't / to / outside
   _____
   _____

3 excited / are / too / down / they / sit / to
   _____
   _____

4 flat / enough / bigger / rich / weren't / buy / to / they / a
   _____
   _____

5 too / we / watch / tired / to / TV / are
   _____
   _____

6 isn't / travel / old / to / she / enough / alone
   _____
   _____

Writing

4 Circle the correct words.

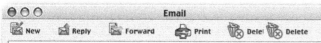

Email

New | Reply | Forward | Print | Delei | Delete

Dear Amazing Kids,

I'm writing to tell you about my best friend Jonah. He's the coolest person I know, and I think he should be the 'Amazing Kid of the Month' winner.

Jonah moved to this country from Africa two years ago. When he first came to our school, he didn't speak any English. **(1)** However / Although, he has tried so hard that he now speaks and writes in English nearly as well as most of his classmates. **(2)** Apart from / Whereas doing well in English, Jonah is good at maths and science.

(3) But / In addition to being a great student, Jonah is also a talented swimmer. He joined the school swim team, and in the last competition he succeeded in winning two gold medals!

Jonah is **(4)** both / as well as clever and funny. He often helps me with my maths homework, and he always makes me laugh. I don't know anyone who is as kind and hard-working as Jonah, and that's why I hope you will choose him to be the 'Amazing Kid of the Month'.

Best wishes,

Steven Greeley

> **Remember!**
>
> We can use these connectors to add information.
> both ...and, as well as ...,
> apart from ..., in addition ...
>
> We can use connectors to contrast two different ideas.
> ... but ..., although ...,
> ... whereas ..., however, ...

5 Write an email to the Amazing Kids website about someone you know who is very brave, clever or talented. Explain why you think this person should be the 'Amazing Kid of the Month' winner.

Begin like this:
Dear Amazing Kids,

Paragraph 1
Introduce the person you are going to describe.

Paragraph 2
Explain why he/she is amazing. Describe what he/she has managed to do and how he/she has faced his/her problems.

Paragraph 3
Say what else he/she has succeeded in doing.

Paragraph 4
Sum up why you think he/she should be the 'Amazing Kid of the Month' winner.

Finish like this:
Best wishes

_____ (your full name)

Reading

1 Read the text about Ludwig van Beethoven.

Ludwig van Beethoven was one of the world's greatest musical geniuses. This amazing pianist and composer was born in Bonn, Germany, in 1770. **(1)** _c_ His father, Johan, was a cruel man and a cruel teacher. Johan gave Ludwig his first piano lessons and punished him when he made mistakes. **(2)** ___ Beethoven wrote his first song when he was 11.

Beethoven got his first job playing the organ when he was only twelve. In 1787, he decided to travel to Vienna to meet another remarkable musician, Wolfgang Amadeus Mozart. **(3)** ___ After becoming known as a brilliant pianist, he spent more time writing music. Beethoven would work on a piece until it was just right. **(4)** ___

When he was in his late twenties, Beethoven began to lose his hearing. **(5)** ___ In 1815 he stopped performing as a pianist but he continued composing. Amazingly, he composed some of the world's greatest music, such as his Ninth Symphony, when he couldn't hear anything at all! Beethoven wrote symphonies, concertos and one opera. He died in Vienna in 1827.

2 Complete the text with these sentences.

a We still don't know if he succeeded in meeting or studying with him.

b It became worse and worse in the years that followed.

c Beethoven had an unhappy childhood.

d Sometimes it took years, but it would be perfect when he finished it.

e He also woke him up late at night to practise.

Vocabulary

3 Choose the correct answers.

1 This time next week, I'll be working at the ___ radio station, WKRP!
  ⓐ local
  b perfect
  c live

2 Our baby will have a fantastic ___ and when he grows up, he'll be a doctor!
  a event
  b task
  c childhood

3 Dad got a new job – he became the ___ of the new village school.
  a caretaker
  b blogger
  c sculptor

4 Stella is going to do a three-year ___ in fashion design at a New York college.
  a occupation
  b career
  c course

5 I'll ___ my name and number and you can call me tomorrow.
  a get through
  b put down
  c take on

6 Did she do it ___ purpose or was it an accident?
  a in
  b on
  c at

7 My four-year-old cousin is really good at doing maths problems – she's a(n) ___!
  a politician
  b artist
  c genius

8 ___ my advice – go to university and get a good education.
  a Give
  b Have
  c Take

9 The boat began to ___ and people started shouting.
  a sink
  b pour
  c crash

10 Is a ___ in journalism one of the qualifications for this job?
  a career
  b degree
  c salary

11 ___ the age of seventy, Katsusuke Yanagisawa climbed Mount Everest!
  a At
  b On
  c For

12 All the members of the ___ are from India.
  a lifeboat
  b crew
  c submarine

Grammar

4 Choose the correct answers.

1 I'm sure you ___ a place at Cornell University.
  a are getting
  b are going to get
  ⓒ will get

2 My class ___ the Tate Gallery next week.
  a is going to visit
  b has visited
  c will have visited

3 What will ___ this time tomorrow?
  a you be doing
  b you have done
  c you doing

4 ___ tell me your name and address, please?
  a Are you going to
  b Will you
  c Do you

5 I ___ your printer! Don't worry, it won't take long.
  a 'll fix
  b 'll be fixing
  c 'll have fixed

6 The engineers ___ the designs by the end of July.
  a have finished
  b will finishing
  c will have finished

7 ___ for you outside the supermarket. Don't be late!
  a I wait
  b I'll be waiting
  c I will have waited

8 You forgot ___ the dog again. It's hungry!
  a feeding
  b to feed
  c feed

9 ___ art history is very interesting.
  a Studying
  b To study
  c Study

10 I decided ___ Mike and ask him to come.
  a email
  b emailing
  c to email

11 I remember ___ you put the tickets in your bag.
  a to have seen
  b seeing
  c to see

12 My uncle started as a painter and went on ___ a sculptor.
  a to become
  b becoming
  c become

7

Vocabulary

1 **Complete the sentences with these words.**

confident   demonstrate   martial   memory   mind   stressed

1 Judo and karate are _____martial_____ arts.

2 The Roman poet Juvenal first said that we should have 'a healthy _____ in a healthy body'.

3 I will now _____ how the printer works. Watch carefully!

4 Relax! Why are you so _____?

5 Margaret can do anything. She's the most _____ person I know.

6 I can't remember names. My _____ isn't as good as it used to be.

2 **Match.**

1 I've joined   a fit by cycling to work.
2 Don't forget to take   b the local gym.
3 My mum keeps   c weight if I exercise?
4 Harry caught a   d bad cold at the weekend.
5 I don't think going on a   e diet is a good idea.
6 Will I lose   f your pills, will you Grandma?

3 **Circle the correct words.**

Are you feeling **(1)** stressed / confident and tired all the time? Do you spend too much time sitting in front of your computer eating snacks? Do you want to **(2)** lose / take weight but don't want to **(3)** catch / go on a diet? Do you think it's time to get fit? Why don't you **(4)** demonstrate / join *Power Gym*? You can do gymnastics, play **(5)** hockey / martial arts or swim in our indoor pool. What are you waiting for? **(6)** Exercise / Keep your mind and body! Be healthy!

Open 9 am – 9 pm every day of the week!

Grammar

4 **Choose the correct answers.**

1 You can leave it here ___.
  (a) until you come back
  b until you came back

2 We can join the gym ___.
  a next week
  b last week

3 We couldn't find the ball ___.
  a until tomorrow.
  b when we looked for it

4 She can cycle to school ___.
  a when her arm is better
  b a few years ago

5 They couldn't buy the CD because ___.
  a they didn't have enough money.
  b they don't have enough money.

6 I can't talk because ___.
  a I had a sore throat
  b I have a sore throat

5 **Complete the sentences with the correct form of** be able to **and the verbs in brackets.**

1 I'm sorry but I _____ *haven't been able to find* _____ (find) your pills yet.

2 Mary _____ (give) Jean any advice because she didn't know anything about diets.

3 I _____ (open) the door. I think this must be the wrong key.

4 _____ (Jack/leave) the hospital tomorrow afternoon?

5 I _____ (come) to soccer practice tomorrow because I have to go to the dentist's.

6 She _____ (walk) when she was only ten months old.

6 **Look at the pictures and write** T **(true) or** F **(false).**

| 1 | 2 | 3 |
| 4 | 5 | 6 |

1 She can go to school.   `F`
2 They can carry the box.   ☐
3 The boy is able to run faster than the girl.   ☐
4 She is able to cycle to school.   ☐
5 He can't stand the noise.   ☐
6 She was able to win the race.   ☐

49

Vocabulary

1 Complete the crossword.

Across

1 The people from the village say that an evil _____spirit_____ lives in the forest.

3 I can't stand this _____. Let's go for a swim.

5 Don't walk around with _____ feet – there's broken glass on the floor.

7 Do Japanese _____ live in temples?

Down

2 You've got time to _____. The competition is next month.

4 I have _____ in you – you can win the race.

6 Losing my job is my worst _____.

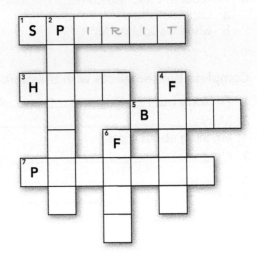

2 Match.

1 Are the children tired?

2 Are you hungry?

3 Is Mum angry?

4 Was Johnny scared?

5 Did you use to be thin?

a Yes, he was terrified!

b Yes, I used to be skinny!

c Yes, I'm starving!

d Yes, she's furious!

e Yes, they're exhausted!

3 Complete the dialogues with these words.

out over up up with

1 A: I'm terrified of spiders!
   B: That's silly. You really have to get ___over___ your fear of them.

2 A: I can't work _____ how much food I will need for the party.
   B: How many people have you invited?

3 A: Did Jim come to dinner last night?
   B: Yes, but he turned _____ late, as usual.

4 A: I've come up _____ an idea – we can rent bikes.
   B: You can't be serious! The village is 50 kilometres away.

5 A: I might have the fish or the chicken.
   B: Fine! But you've got one minute to make _____ your mind!

Grammar

4 **Complete the sentences with** must **or** can't.

1 You haven't had anything to eat all day. You ___must___ be hungry.
2 He _____ be a professional singer. He's got a horrible voice.
3 Those coals are very hot! His feet _____ hurt!
4 She _____ know a lot about science. She has read lots of scientific magazines and books.
5 That _____ be Bob. He won't be back from New York until next week.
6 You _____ be exhausted. You slept for twelve hours last night!

5 **Circle the correct answers**

1 Jackie must / may not be rich. She's a famous film star.
2 These can't / might not be my glasses. My glasses are black.
3 Andy may / must be going to the festival, but he hasn't decided yet.
4 Jill is your best friend! You can't / must have her email address!
5 She isn't answering her phone. She might / can't be asleep.
6 I might not / must not invite Sam to my party. I don't like him very much.

6 **Choose the correct answers.**

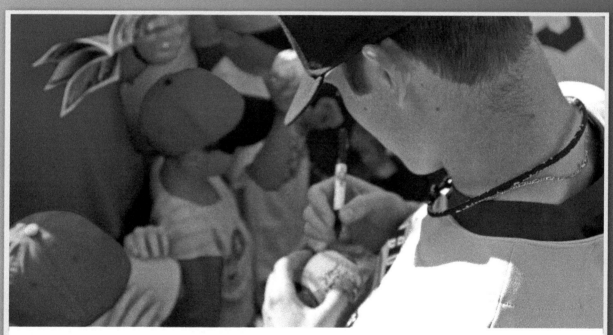

Mark: My dad said that he **(1)** ___ take me to a baseball game this weekend.
Brenda: Really? That's brilliant! He **(2)** ___ be very pleased with you for some reason.
Mark: He is! I washed the car for him and I did the shopping too. He **(3)** ___ get us really good tickets and I **(4)** ___ get the chance to meet my favourite player!
Brenda: You **(5)** ___ be serious. You can't talk to the players during a game!
Mark: That's true. But I **(6)** ___ be able to talk to him after the game!
Brenda: Can you ask him for an autograph?

1	a	must	b	might	c	can't
2	a	might	b	can't	c	must
3	a	can't	b	may not	c	may
4	a	might not	b	might	c	can't
5	a	may not	b	can't	c	mustn't
6	a	might	b	might not	c	must

7 Lesson 3

Vocabulary

1 Complete the sentences with do, feel or make.

1 You shouldn't _____feel_____ nervous – you've practised a lot and you'll win.
2 He should _____ an effort to exercise more.
3 Why don't you _____ the best you can and then see what happens?
4 I always _____ a list of the things I need before going to the supermarket.
5 Don't _____ upset – you've done nothing wrong.
6 You shouldn't feel stressed before you _____ a test.

Grammar

2 Rewrite the sentences with the words given in brackets and any other words that are necessary.

1 Doing more exercise is a good idea. (should)
You _____should do_____ more exercise.
2 Don't listen to what your 'friends' say. (must)
You _____ to what your 'friends' say.
3 It isn't necessary to go to school today. (have)
We _____ to school today.
4 It's important that you try to be yourself. (ought)
You _____ to be yourself.
5 It isn't necessary for Stella to go on a diet. (doesn't)
Stella _____ on a diet if she doesn't want to.
6 You have to eat less food if you want to lose weight. (must)
You _____ less food if you want to lose weight.

Express yourself!

3 Look at the pictures and write the correct sentences.

Do you think we should eat healthier food?

They'd better not go to work.

What do you think I should eat?

Why don't you join our gym?

They'd better not go to work.

Writing

4 **Read the letter and answer the questions.**

Dear Aunt Agatha,

This is my first year in secondary school, and I hate it! My marks are awful, and my mum and dad are always angry with me.

The problem is that they think I'm not trying hard enough. Well, that's not true! I study for two or three hours every day, I do my homework, and I like most of the school subjects, especially maths and science! What's wrong with me? I'm beginning to think that I'm stupid! When I get up in the morning, I feel sad because I have to go to school.

I need help. What should I do?

Linda, 12

Remember!

We can use these phrases to ask for advice.
What should I do?
Please tell me how I can ...?

We can use these phrases to give advice.
I suggest that you should ...
Why don't you ...?

We can use these phrases to end a letter of advice.
I hope you are able to ...
I'm sure you will ...
Good luck!

1 Why are Linda's parents angry with her?
   Because her marks are awful.

2 What do Linda's parents think?
   _____

3 How long does Linda study every day?
   _____

4 How does Linda feel before she goes to school in the morning?
   _____

5 What advice could you give her?
   _____
   _____
   _____

5 **Write a reply to the letter in 4, giving advice to Linda. Don't forget to use the phrases in the Remember! box for giving advice. Use this plan to help you.**

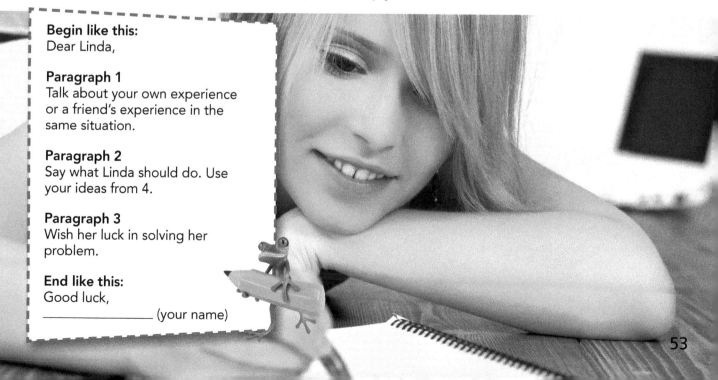

Begin like this:
Dear Linda,

Paragraph 1
Talk about your own experience or a friend's experience in the same situation.

Paragraph 2
Say what Linda should do. Use your ideas from 4.

Paragraph 3
Wish her luck in solving her problem.

End like this:
Good luck,

_____ (your name)

8 Lesson 1

Vocabulary

1 Match.

1 portrait ☐ c
2 landscape ☐
3 graffiti ☐
4 exhibition ☐
5 frame ☐
6 handwriting ☐

2 The words in bold are in the wrong sentences. Write the correct words.

1 The yellow **copy** in the painting is the sun. _____ dot _____

2 My grandma was a woman of great **background** – everybody found her very attractive. _____

3 Wow! Purple, orange, red and green … that's a very **helpful** hat, Dad! _____

4 This artist always uses pale colours on a dark **beauty**. _____

5 This isn't a real Miró painting – it's a **dot**! _____

6 He always tidies his bedroom and puts his toys away – he's very **colourful**. _____

3 Write the missing letters.

1 A large building where people can see famous pieces of art.
g a l l e r y

2 A special light used when taking photographs indoors.
f _ _ _ _

3 A hard metal that has got a red-brown colour.
b _ _ _ _ _

4 When you want to keep someone safe from danger.
p _ _ _ _ _ _ _ _

5 A colour that is strong and easy to see.
b _ _ _ _ _

6 The shapes, lines and colours on something.
p _ _ _ _ _ _

Grammar

4 Complete the paragraph with the Present Simple passive of the verbs in brackets.

Welcome to the Louvre Museum in Paris, France!

- The Louvre Museum **(1)** _____is visited_____ (visit) by about 15,000 people every day!
- Leonardo da Vinci's famous painting, the *Mona Lisa*, **(2)** _____ (keep) behind special protective glass in the museum. The painting **(3)** _____ (see) by 6 million people every year.
- Films about art history **(4)** _____ (show) at the museum – the programme changes every four months.
- Sculptures and paintings **(5)** _____ (look after) by more than 2,000 people who work there!
- Museum tickets **(6)** _____ (sold) at the museum or at the Paris Tourist Office. Children **(7)** _____ (given) a special price.

5 Choose the correct answers.

1 Was this photo ___ when we were on holiday in France?
  a take
  b taken
  c took

2 The athletes ___ trained by a professional coach.
  a are
  b was
  c have

3 It ___ painted two hundred years ago.
  a weren't
  b wasn't
  c didn't

4 We were taught how to paint landscapes ___ our art teacher.
  a of
  b from
  c by

5 They ___ expected to be here at six o'clock.
  a is
  b are
  c am

6 Were the best statues ___ by Michelangelo?
  a created
  b create
  c creating

6 Rewrite the sentences with the words given in brackets and any other words necessary.

1 Vincent van Gogh painted *Sunflowers*. (by)
Sunflowers _____was painted by_____ Vincent van Gogh.

2 They didn't tell us that the art gallery was closed. (were)
We _____ that the art gallery was closed.

3 A farmer found an ancient sculpture on his land. (by)
An ancient sculpture _____ a farmer on his land.

4 Unfortunately, my friends didn't invite me to the party. (was)
Unfortunately, I _____ to the party by my friends.

5 Thousands of people visited the exhibition. (by)
The exhibition _____ thousands of people.

55

Vocabulary

1 Complete the dialogues with these words.

charts   contract   film   habits   marketing   record

1 A: Why are you so excited, Alex?
   B: They are going to _____film_____ our concert tonight!

2 A: What song are you listening to? It's awful!
   B: Are you crazy? This song is number one in the UK music _____!

3 A: What do you know about the *Arctic Monkeys*?
   B: I know they signed their first _____ in 2005.

4 A: Have you got any plans for a new CD?
   B: Yes, I'm going to _____ my new songs in a studio in New York.

5 A: Why are they giving away free CDs?
   B: They want to advertise their new single and it's part of their _____ plan.

6 A: More and more people shop online.
   B: That's true. The Internet has changed our shopping _____.

2 Choose the correct answers.

1 I like rock music, but I'm not a lover ___ hip hop.
   a to
   b on
   c of ⊙

2 Money hasn't changed my attitude ___ life.
   a of
   b to
   c for

3 Can we go somewhere else? I'm not very keen ___ jazz music.
   a on
   b in
   c over

4 There's a need ___ more and better trained staff.
   a of
   b for
   c with

5 Joe thinks he's an expert ___ country music.
   a to
   b for
   c on

6 Were their first songs recorded ___ CDs?
   a on
   b in
   c at

3 Write P (Person), K (Kinds of music) or S (Song-related words).

1	guitarist	P	6	drummer	☐
2	single	☐	7	classical	☐
3	lyrics	☐	8	hit	☐
4	fan	☐	9	bassist	☐
5	rap	☐	10	hip hop	☐

Grammar

4 **Choose the correct answers.**

1 Songs ___ for her new CD.
   (a) were being recorded
   b were recording

2 Tickets for the concert ___ at the Information Centre.
   a can be bought
   b can buy

3 Classical music ___ by the orchestra now.
   a was being played
   b is being played

4 George Star's new programme ___ on TV next Saturday evening.
   a has been shown
   b will be shown

5 The winners of the talent competition ___ a place in a famous music college.
   a had be offered
   b had been offered

6 The film star ___ by a journalist yesterday.
   a was being interviewed
   b was interviewing

5 **Write sentences with the correct form of the passive voice.**

1 her new single / record / at the moment
   Her new single is being recorded at the moment.

2 the book / might / make / into a film
   _____

3 the songs / not upload / onto their website / every day
   _____

4 the winner of the talent competition / not choose / yet
   _____

5 ? / the contract / sign / last week
   _____

6 live music / play / at the party / next week
   _____

6 **Complete the interview with the correct form of the verbs in brackets in the passive voice.**

Interviewer:	Today, I'm speaking to Carol King. Carol is the marketing manager of the local talent show, and she is very excited about it. Tell us all about the show, Carol.
Carol:	This talent show is going to be the biggest and the best yet, Peter! It **(1)** _is going to be recorded_ (record) live, and I believe it **(2)** _____ (watch) by hundreds of viewers!
Interviewer:	And what **(3)** _____ (do) so far, Carol?
Carol:	Well, the singers' and dancers' costumes **(4)** _____ (already/design), but they **(5)** _____ (not make) yet. The lights and microphones **(6)** _____ (test) at the moment, and the presenter of the show **(7)** _____ (choose) next week.
Interviewer:	It sounds like everything **(8)** _____ (prepare), Carol. We wish you lots of luck with the show!
Carol:	Thanks, Peter.

Vocabulary

1 Circle the correct words.

			Email			
New | Reply | Forward | Print | Delete | Send & Receive

Hi Mandy!

I had to write and tell you my news. I'm going to have the **(1)** first / lead role in the school play this year! The rest of the roles will be **(2)** played / given by my classmates. I had to go through three **(3)** auditions / productions before I was given the role. I am very **(4)** professional / nervous about it because I've never been **(5)** to / on stage before! I like acting, and I'm going to try hard and make sure my **(6)** performance / remake is good. The play is a comedy, and I hope you will be able to come and see me.

Write soon,

Betty

Express yourself!

2 Look at the pictures and write questions.

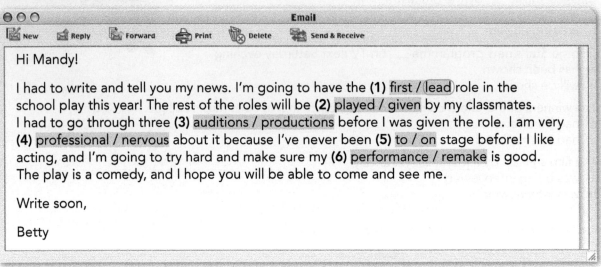

What was your trip like?

? / what / your trip / like

? / what / it like / to be / 70

? / what / you / think of / the party

? / what / your sandwich / like

? / what / you / think of / the film

Speaking

3 Work with a partner. Take it in turns to tell each other what things have or haven't been done before the art gallery opening. Use the passive voice and the prompts below.

1	door / fix	✓	**3**	flowers / buy	✗	**5**	paintings / put on walls ✓
2	floors / clean	✓	**4**	food / put on tables	✗	**6**	invitations / send ✓

Writing

4 Look at the two paragraph plans for a review. Which one is better?

Paragraph 1 – name of show, name of composer, names of all the actors and singers
Paragraph 2 – what happened in each scene of the show
Paragraph 3 – reasons why you didn't enjoy the show
Paragraph 4 – description of the setting and costumes

Paragraph 1 – name of show, when you saw it, name of theatre
Paragraph 2 – general information about the show
Paragraph 3 – focus on one or two things about the show (the acting/music/the costumes/other)
Paragraph 4 – recommendation

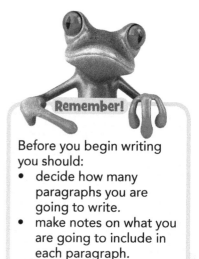

Remember!

Before you begin writing you should:
- decide how many paragraphs you are going to write.
- make notes on what you are going to include in each paragraph.

5 Read the review and put the paragraphs in the correct order. Then decide which of the two paragraph plans the writer has used.

☐
I recommend *Magic on Ice* to anyone who wants to have a fantastic night out! It is brilliant for all the family – children and adults. At the end of the show, you won't want to leave the theatre!

1
My friends and I went to see *Magic on Ice* at the Odeon Theatre two weeks ago. It was a very exciting experience!

☐
What I liked best about the show was the magician's performance. He was a wonderful skater and a talented magician at the same time. He did the most amazing magic tricks on ice! He pulled rabbits out of hats and turned handkerchiefs into birds.

☐
Magic on Ice is an ice-skating show with clowns, magicians and jugglers. It's like going to a circus, only better! It was first performed in New York in 2005, and the ice skaters have been travelling around the world ever since. It's a very entertaining show because it's both funny and spectacular.

6 Write a review of a play or performance which you have seen. Before you begin your writing, make a plan with notes for each paragraph. Use the correct plan in 4 to help you.

Reading

1 Read the text about Cadillac Ranch.

What is art? Some art lovers think art is a famous portrait by da Vinci or a well-known landscape by Monet. Others think that graffiti on walls or the cars at Cadillac Ranch in the USA are forms of art too.

Cadillac Ranch is made up of ten junk Cadillac cars – old cars that their owners didn't want any more. In 1974, three men from San Francisco, who were members of an art group, decided to use those Cadillac cars and create a place of modern art in a big field in Amarillo, Texas.

The Cadillacs are half-buried in the ground and they've been painted lots of different bright colours! People who visit the ranch are invited to bring paint and spray the Cadillacs. Every day, the colour of the cars, and the graffiti written on them, is different!

The Cadillacs have now been in the ground as pieces of art longer than they were on the road! Songs have been sung about Cadillac Ranch, and TV programmes and films have been made there. It is art, and it is an exhibition that you need to see to believe! Go and see ... and take your paint with you!

2 Write T (true) or F (false).

1 Monet and da Vinci were both artists. `T`

2 There are ten cars at Cadillac Ranch. ☐

3 The men who started Cadillac Ranch were from Texas. ☐

4 People cannot write on the cars at Cadillac Ranch. ☐

5 Cadillac Ranch has been on television. ☐

Vocabulary

3 Choose the correct answers.

1 You've put on weight. You need to ___ a diet.
   a go on
   b catch
   c keep

2 He didn't have lunch and now he's ___!
   a starving
   b skinny
   c bare

3 Her first ___ went to number one on the US charts.
   a fan
   b habit
   c single

4 Mum couldn't sleep last night and now she is ___.
   a furious
   b terrified
   c exhausted

5 These ___ of the Miró painting were made by an art thief.
   a copies
   b scenes
   c charts

6 Can we take photos at night without turning on the ___ on this camera?
   a light
   b flash
   c frame

7 Have no ___, Superman is here!
   a mind
   b fear
   c faith

8 He's a world expert ___ modern art.
   a on
   b of
   c for

9 First the instructor ___ the new moves and then he let the class try them.
   a prepared
   b kicked
   c demonstrated

10 He signed his first ___ with a record company when he was fifteen.
   a contract
   b lyrics
   c hit

11 They can't ___ a gym because they have no free time.
   a go
   b join
   c take

12 This famous painting is kept in a ___ glass frame – nobody wants it to be damaged.
   a bright
   b protective
   c helpful

Grammar

4 Choose the correct answers.

1 ___ to get tickets for the rap concert?
   a Could you
   b Can you
   c Were you able

2 He ___ eat his breakfast because he felt ill.
   a isn't able to
   b can't
   c couldn't

3 Their concerts ___ by their fans.
   a are often recording
   b they often record
   c are often recorded

4 Loud music ___ be played after eleven o'clock.
   a could
   b mustn't
   c must

5 This ___ be the right way to do it, but I'm not sure.
   a might
   b can't
   c must

6 The huge statue ___ by an American artist called Seward Johnson.
   a was created
   b created
   c was creating

7 That ___ be my mobile phone – mine is white.
   a can't
   b mustn't
   c might not

8 Who was this portrait painted ___?
   a in
   b by
   c at

9 The song ___ by a famous orchestra.
   a was being played
   b was playing
   c played

10 I think you ___ to apologise to your friend.
   a ought
   b should
   c shouldn't

11 She ___ love hip hop music – she listens to it all the time.
   a can
   b might
   c must

12 We ___ go out — we can stay in and listen to my new CD.
   a couldn't
   b mustn't
   c don't have to

61

Vocabulary

1 Look at the pictures and write the missing letters.

f l i p p e r s

r _ _ _ _ _ _ _

g _ _ _ _ _ _

p _ _ _ _ _ _ _ _ _ _

g _ _ _ _ _ _

w _ _ _ _ _ _ _ _ _ _ _

2 Complete the sentences with these words.

life jacket   original   parachute   raise   sunbathing   wetsuit

1 Having a talent competition is not a very _____original_____ idea. Can you think of something else?
2 It's dangerous to go jet skiing without wearing a _____.
3 The man jumped from the plane and his _____ helped him fall slowly and safely to the ground.
4 If I don't wear this _____, I won't be able to stay in the cold ocean water for very long.
5 My favourite part of a holiday is _____ on the beach.
6 You can _____ money for charity by having a concert at school.

3 Match.

1 Why have you put your goggles and flippers in the car?
2 Why is your skin red, Mum?
3 Do you know where the lifejackets are?
4 What do I do after I jump from the plane?
5 Why don't you try scuba diving?

a Wait for one minute and then open your parachute.
b Because I'm going snorkelling this afternoon.
c Yes. They are under the benches at the back of the boat.
d I'm not a very adventurous person.
e I've been sunbathing all morning.

Grammar

4 **Circle the correct words.**

1 If we won't wear / (don't wear) flippers, we won't be able to swim fast.
2 If you wear a wetsuit in the water, your body is staying / stays warm.
3 She can't / must go paragliding if she doesn't have lessons first.
4 If you go / will go kite surfing, the instructor will tell you what to do first.
5 You won't raise enough money if you don't / won't advertise the event.
6 If he wears goggles in the water, he will be able to see / is seeing lots of fish.

5 **Complete the first conditional sentences with the verbs in brackets.**

1 We _____ will feel _____ (feel) proud if we raise lots of money for charity.
2 If I exercise more, _____ (I/lose) weight?
3 She will get wet if she _____ (go) cycling in the rain.
4 You _____ (not be) safe if you don't listen to my instructions.
5 What _____ (you/do) if you don't find skiing equipment to rent?
6 If the weather is nice tomorrow, I _____ (do) my very first parachute jump.
7 He can't become an instructor if he _____ (not pass) the exam.

6 **Write sentences using the first conditional.**

1 if / you / not wear / a helmet / you / may / hurt / your head
   If you don't wear a helmet, you may hurt your head.
2 I / feel / proud of her / if / she / win / the competition
   _____
3 your hands / get cold / unless / you / wear / warm gloves
   _____
4 if / they / wear / their life jackets / they / be / safe on the boat
   _____
5 if / you / not wear / good walking boots / you / may / fall down the cliff
   _____
6 unless / he / train / hard / he / not be able to / become a champion
   _____

Vocabulary

1 Match.

1 roll down a hill	☑ f	
2 score a goal	☐	
3 beat a competitor	☐	
4 aim to hit something	☐	
5 land on the ground	☐	
6 hit a ball	☐	

2 Complete the sentences with these words.

creator   diameter   facing   harness   typical   water slide

1 Please draw a circle five centimetres in _____diameter_____.
2 If you went paragliding, you would have to wear a safety _____.
3 The children's hair and clothes are wet – they've been on the _____.
4 A _____ baseball weighs about 140 grams.
5 Was the _____ of this extreme sport from Germany?
6 The two men sat working at desks _____ each other.

3 Circle the correct words.

1 Don't forget to warm up / out before you exercise.
2 She had to drop up / out of the race because she hurt her arm.
3 If she ran faster, she could catch off / up with the other runners.
4 James is very fit. He must work in / out at the gym every day.
5 We haven't got much time – the match kicks off / on at one o'clock.

Grammar

4 Complete the second conditional sentences with the verbs in brackets.

1 If I were you, I ___would wear___ (wear) a lifejacket.

2 She would go scuba diving if she _____ (not be) so scared.

3 He would go to the gym every day if he _____ (have) the time.

4 If I _____ (be) you, I wouldn't give up tennis.

5 If they knew how dangerous it was, they _____ (not go) paragliding.

6 I _____ (take part) in the race if I had the right equipment.

7 If you had the chance, _____ (you/try) kite surfing?

5 Choose the correct answers.

1 If I liked extreme sports, I ___ BASE jumping.
  a would try
  b wouldn't try
  c had to try

2 I ___ him the photos if I had his email address.
  a would send
  b send
  c will send

3 If I were you, I ___ go cycling without a helmet.
  a wasn't
  b didn't
  c wouldn't

4 What would you do if you ___ eighteen years old again?
  a are
  b were
  c would be

5 If you ___ Australia, would you go snorkelling?
  a visit
  b would visit
  c visited

6 If you had €200, what ___ it on?
  a will you spend
  b would you spend
  c did you spend

6 Complete the dialogues with the second conditional. Use these verbs.

be go have jump know rent

1 **A:** Mr Smith thinks I cheated in the test.
  B: If I _____were_____ you, I'd talk to him about it.

2 **A:** If you _____ the chance, would you go rafting?
  B: No! I don't like water sports.

3 **A:** If we lived near a beach, I _____ swimming every day.
  B: You would be very fit.

4 **A:** If I _____ out of a plane, I would feel terrified.
  B: So would I if I didn't have a parachute!

5 **A:** If I were you, I _____ equipment from the club.
  B: I don't think I can afford it.

6 **A:** The garden has flooded!
  B: Oh no! If Dad were here, he _____ what to do.

Lesson 3

Vocabulary

1 Complete the sentences with these words.

bounce   contestants   finishing line   opponent   prize   tradition

1 Harry crossed the _____*finishing line*_____ five seconds before Jamal.
2 My sister was one of the _____ in the talent competition.
3 Drinking tea in the afternoon is a _____ in Britain.
4 What's the _____ for the winner of the competition?
5 Stop that! You mustn't _____ up and down on the sofa.
6 His _____ in today's match will be a famous tennis champion.

Grammar

2 Circle the correct words.

1 If the hill hadn't been so steep, Jerry (wouldn't have) / wouldn't broken his leg while running.
2 If I hadn't read about the cheese-rolling race on the Internet, I wasn't / wouldn't have taken part in it.
3 If you ask / had asked me, I would have given you my skiing equipment.
4 Would they have won the race if they trained / had trained harder?
5 If I had known / knew you were going rafting, I would have come with you.
6 If we had left earlier, we wouldn't have missed / wouldn't miss our flight.
7 If this happened / had happened to you, would you have done the same?

Express yourself!

3 Look at the pictures and complete the sentences using adjectives with numbers.

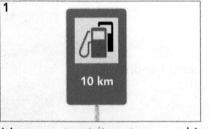

1 It's a _____*ten-kilometre*_____ drive to the next petrol station.

2 This is a _____ note.

3 We are going to have a _____ break.

4 He's carrying a _____ box.

Writing

4 Read the email and replace the formal phrases in bold with these informal phrases. Add capital letters and punctuation as necessary.

for ages   guess what   ~~hi Jake~~   how's it going   let me know
really cool   what have you been up to   write soon

Remember!

We should use informal language in a letter or email to a friend. For example:
How's it going?
What have you been up to?
Let me know …
Guess what?
for ages
… cool …

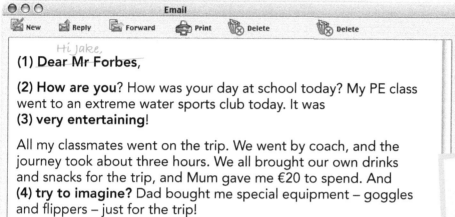

```
  ○○○                    Email
  New    Reply   Forward   Print   Delete      Delete
```

Hi Jake,

(1) Dear Mr Forbes,

(2) How are you? How was your day at school today? My PE class went to an extreme water sports club today. It was **(3) very entertaining**!

All my classmates went on the trip. We went by coach, and the journey took about three hours. We all brought our own drinks and snacks for the trip, and Mum gave me €20 to spend. And **(4) try to imagine?** Dad bought me special equipment – goggles and flippers – just for the trip!

The extreme sports club is near a beautiful beach, and you can choose from a number of different water sports. You can go paragliding, scuba diving or windsurfing. There are instructors there to tell you what you can and can't do. I had wanted to go snorkelling **(5) for an extremely long time**, and my dream finally came true! It was great fun and more exciting than I thought it would be!

What about you? **(6) What have you been doing lately?** Have you been on any interesting school trips recently? Send me an email and **(7) inform me.**

(8) Please reply in the near future!

Ralph

5 Imagine you went to an extreme sports club on a recent school trip. Write an email to a friend about it. Don't forget to use informal language. Use this plan to help you.

Begin your email like this:
Hi _____ (your friend's name)!

Paragraph 1
Ask your friend one or two questions. Mention where you went for the school trip and say when it took place.

Paragraph 2
Give details of the journey and say what you took on the trip.

Paragraph 3
Describe the place you visited and what you did there. Give details of one thing you really liked doing.

Paragraph 4
Ask your friend if he/she has been on any interesting school trips. Ask him/her to send you an email.

End your email with one of these phrases:
Bye for now! / Write soon!
_____ (your name)

67

10 Lesson 1

Vocabulary

1 Look at the pictures and write the correct phrases.

> arrest a criminal   call the police
> put in prison   rob a bank   steal a car

___arrest a criminal___

2 Choose the correct answers.

1 The same man has ___ three crimes.
   (a) committed
   b plotted

2 The woman was probably ___ by her uncle.
   a related
   b murdered

3 I haven't ___ the law! You must believe me!
   a broken
   b robbed

4 The soldiers ___ the castle and killed the king's enemy.
   a blew up
   b blew down

5 How many people have been ___ at the Tower of London?
   a haunted
   b executed

6 When was your bag ___?
   a robbed
   b stolen

3 Write the missing letters.

1 When you kill someone, usually by law.
e _x_ _e_ _c_ _u_ _t_ _e_

2 Someone whose job is to protect a place or person.
g _ _ _ _

3 When you steal money from a person or bank.
r _ _

4 Something that is strange and frightening.
s _ _ _ _ _

5 How we describe a building which people believe is visited by ghosts.
h _ _ _ _ _ _

6 Someone who is kept in prison.
p _ _ _ _ _ _ _

Grammar

4 **Complete the sentences with the correct form of the verbs in brackets.**

1 I didn't call the police.
I wish I _____ *had called* _____ the police. (call)

2 They robbed my best friend's house.
I wish they _____ my best friend's house. (not rob)

3 We have broken the law.
If only we _____ the law. (not break)

4 I'm not a famous detective.
If only I _____ a famous detective. (be)

5 He left his front door open.
He wishes he _____ his front door open. (not leave)

6 She's not careful with her things.
If only she _____ careful with her things. (be)

5 **Complete the sentences with the correct form of the verbs in brackets.**

1 I wish I _____ *hadn't taken* _____ (not take) the girl's MP3 player.

2 I wish she _____ (not have) a dog with her that day.

3 I wish the dog _____ (not chase) me when I took her MP3 player.

4 If only I _____ (not slip) on the ice.

5 I wish the dog _____ (not bite) me!

6 **Circle the correct words.**

If only I **(1)** didn't look / hadn't looked out my window last night at eight o'clock. It was so embarrassing! I saw a fair-haired young man trying to get into the house across the road through the front window. I was sure he was a criminal!

I ran across the road quickly … but I wish I **(2)** had stayed / stayed in my sitting room. I wish I **(3)** didn't shout / hadn't shouted at him. An old woman opened the door and she started laughing. She said, 'I wish you **(4)** saw / could see your face now! You look terrified!' and then the young man started laughing too. If only I **(5)** understood / had understood what they thought was so funny.

Then the old woman said, 'This is my son. If only he **(6)** hasn't / hadn't forgotten his keys, this wouldn't have happened.' I couldn't say a word. I stood there and thought to myself, 'I wish I **(7)** didn't make / hadn't made a fool of myself!'

69

Vocabulary

1 Label the pictures with these words.

burglar   court   judge   seal   staircase   theft

staircase

___

___

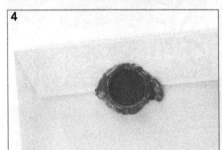
___

___

___

2 Choose the correct answers.

1 There was a murder in the neighbourhood last night. The ___ are on their way and they will question everybody.
   a guards
   b investigators

2 You should never talk to ___! They might be criminals.
   a owners
   b strangers

3 Will the man who took the little girl make ___ with her parents?
   a seal
   b contact

4 The news of the car crash ___ the family.
   a shocked
   b questioned

5 The ___ of the art gallery called the police when he realised the painting had been stolen.
   a detective
   b owner

6 Jessie James was a famous American train ___.
   a robber
   b thief

3 Complete the sentences with these words.

about   for   for   into   of   of

1 He didn't give us the reason _____for_____ his decision.
2 The police officers managed to find the cause _____ the accident.
3 He's the murderer – there's no doubt _____ it.
4 This is the result _____ eating too many sweets.
5 The investigation _____ the crime has been going on for months now.
6 They are still searching _____ the stolen statue.

Grammar

4 **Match.**

1 Nobody helped me.
2 Tina fell off her bicycle.
3 John and I didn't have a nice time.
4 Carl's finger is hurt.
5 Stop arguing with your brother!
6 Mum didn't make the boys' beds.

a We didn't enjoy ourselves.
b Behave yourself!
c They did it themselves.
d She hurt herself.
e He cut himself.
f I did it myself.

5 **Circle the correct words.**

1 Don't walk home by yourself / himself. It's not safe.
2 He hurt himself / herself when he fell down the stairs.
3 Maria doesn't buy clothes – she makes them itself / herself.
4 I keep telling myself / himself not to worry about crime, but I can't help it.
5 We are investigating the theft themselves / ourselves because the police have been no help at all.
6 Does he live in that flat by itself / himself?
7 We can't go with them – they've got to go by themselves / ourselves.

6 **Complete the dialogues with these words.**

himself   itself   myself   ourselves   yourself
yourselves

1 A: I fell off my bike, Mum.
   B: Oh no! Did you hurt ____yourself____?

2 A: Girls, did you behave _____ while we were out?
   B: Yes, we did.

3 A: Was Joe by _____ when the burglar got into the house?
   B: No. Luckily, he had two friends with him.

4 A: There was another burglary in the neighbourhood last night.
   B: Oh no! How can we protect _____ from criminals?

5 A: I can't help you right now. I'm busy.
   B: Fine. I'll do it _____.

6 A: My new TV turns _____ off at 12 o'clock at night.
   B: That's fantastic!

71

Vocabulary

1 Complete the sentences with these words.

break   burst   drop   hear   keep   take

1 _____Take_____ a look at this photo. Is this the man who stole your bag?
2 The burglar tried to _____ into the house through the kitchen window.
3 Visitors to the park will pay fines if they _____ litter.
4 There's a lot of crime in the area. _____ an eye on your bag when you are on the bus or the train.
5 While the police were questioning the young girl, she _____ into tears.
6 I can _____ loud cries coming from the flat downstairs. Should we call the police?

Express yourself!

2 Circle the correct words.

Jason: Hi Helen!

Helen: Hi Jason! Did you hear **(1)** about / for the burglary at the Baileys' house last night? You won't **(2)** believe / hear what happened.

Jason: What?

Helen: Well, the burglar got into the house, took what he wanted to take and then … he cooked himself this huge meal!

Jason: No **(3)** way / matter!

Helen: Yes! And guess **(4)** that / what happened then.

Jason: What?

Helen: Well, after he had finished eating, he decided he was tired. The Baileys came home and found him sleeping on the sofa! He didn't hear them come in, or hear them call the police!

Jason: You must be **(5)** joking / looking! I don't **(6)** believe / feel it!

Helen: It's true! And now the burglar will probably go to prison.

Speaking

3 Talk to your partner about a crime that you have heard about. Explain what happened, who was involved and how it ended.

Writing

4 Read the story and complete the plan with the correct numbers.

Beginning: Paragraph ___
Middle: Paragraph _1_
Paragraph ___
Ending: Paragraph ___

Remember!

A good story should have an introduction, a middle and an ending.

1
My cousin and I knew these 'crimes of art' were happening late at night, so we waited until everyone was sleeping and we climbed out of a window. We were walking through the village looking for the criminal when we saw someone standing in front of a house. He was holding something in his hand. My cousin said, 'He's got a can of paint! That's our man!'

2
Last summer I was staying at my uncle's house in an English village. It's a very small place and there isn't much crime there. Well, there wasn't until then! Someone was spraying graffiti on the front doors of people's houses. My cousin Celia and I decided to investigate!

3
While we were chasing him, I fell and hurt myself. Celia helped me back to her house where her parents were waiting. We were very tired … and they were furious! We told them what had happened, and my uncle asked why we hadn't called the police. I said, 'We thought we could catch him ourselves. But it won't happen again! I've had enough adventures.'

4
We hid behind some trees in the park just opposite the house. We watched as the man went up to the front door and began spraying something on the door. Then Celia jumped up and shouted, 'Stop! Police!' The criminal took one look at us and burst out laughing. Then he ran away into the park.

5 Write a story that ends with the words, 'I've had enough adventures.' Use the questions in the plan to help you.

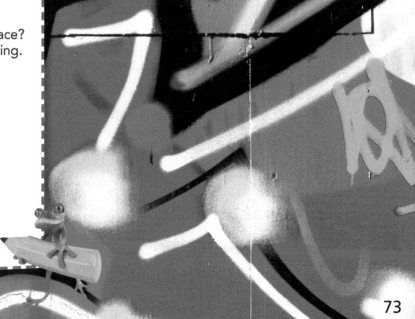

Paragraph 1: Introduction
Describe the situation.
When did the events in the story take place?
Where is the story set? Describe the setting.
Who are the main characters?

Paragraphs 2 and 3: Middle
Describe the action.
What happened first?
What was the result of the action?
What happened next?
Did something go wrong? If so, what?

Paragraph 4: Ending
Describe how the story ended.
Say how you/the main characters felt.
How do you/they feel about it now?

Reading

1 Read the text about the Marathon de Sables.

If you're looking for a real challenge, the Marathon de Sables has got what you want! This six-day race takes place every March or April. It's called 'the most extreme foot race on Earth' because runners travel across 251 kilometres of the burning Sahara Desert in Morocco. It's like running in six regular marathons in temperatures of up to 40°C!

As you can imagine, the race is very difficult – two racers have died during the event since it started in 1986. Racers need to carry food and everything else they might need in their backpacks. They are given water and tents by the organisers. Competitors pay more than £2,500 to take part in the race! That money helps pay for the 400 members of staff, doctors, nurses, and the buses, helicopters and planes that are used during the marathon.

Since the race began, the Moroccan Lahcen Ahansal has won ten times and his brother Mohammed Ahansal three times. One competitor who is never likely to win, however, is Englishman Paul Roberts. He has decided to make the race even tougher by combining it with extreme ironing! He will carry his ironing board and iron clothes during the race.

2 Write R (Right), W (Wrong) or DS (Doesn't say).

1 The race takes place in the same month every year. ☐ W

2 The Marathon de Sables first took place in 1986. ☐

3 Two racers have died because they had no water. ☐

4 It's expensive to take part in the race. ☐

5 Lahcen Ahansal has won the race fewer times than his brother. ☐

6 Extreme ironing is an English invention. ☐

Vocabulary

3 Choose the correct answers.

1 If I go ___ at the weekend, I'll need a new mask.
a rafting
ⓑ snorkelling
c kite surfing

2 If only I hadn't ___ the law! I wouldn't be in the police station now.
a searched
b questioned
c broken

3 They wish they hadn't ___ the statue. They're in big trouble now!
a stolen
b robbed
c murdered

4 When he goes mountain climbing, he always wears ___ to protect his hands.
a flippers
b goggles
c gloves

5 'What is the ___ of a zorb ball?'
'I think it's about three metres.'
a harness
b diameter
c equipment

6 If we get one more point, we will ___ the other team!
a beat
b raise
c score

7 Do men or women ___ more crimes?
a call
b commit
c arrest

8 If you don't ___ before you exercise, you'll be sorry later.
a warm up
b kick off
c work out

9 The police ___ asked the manager where he was at the time of the robbery.
a prisoner
b investigator
c guard

10 Unless you wear a ___ when you go diving, you'll get very cold.
a wetsuit
b parachute
c life jacket

11 Luckily, Mr Smith wasn't by himself when the ___ broke the window and got into his house.
a owner
b judge
c burglar

12 There is no doubt ___ it – she killed the man herself!
a for
b of
c about

Grammar

4 Choose the correct answers.

1 Mike won't be safe ___ wears a life jacket.
ⓐ unless he
b if he
c unless he doesn't

2 If you ___, you won't be cold.
a would dress warmly
b dress warmly
c will dress warmly

3 You ___ faster if you wear flippers.
a swim
b are swimming
c swam

4 If he ___ older, he could go zorbing with his sister.
a were
b is
c would be

5 You wouldn't have injured yourself if you ___ a harness.
a wear
b do wear
c had worn

6 I hope the children will behave ___ at the museum.
a them
b themselves
c by themselves

7 If I had enough money, I ___ kite surfing lessons.
a would take
b took
c take

8 I made ___ a delicious sandwich earlier.
a yourself
b itself
c myself

9 ___ I hadn't stolen that money!
a If only
b If
c Unless

10 I wish we ___ the other team in yesterday's match.
a would beat
b will beat
c had beaten

11 Mario wrote this detective story by ___. Isn't he clever?
a herself
b himself
c themselves

12 I wish I ___ brave enough to go bungee jumping.
a be
b were
c am

Lesson 1

Vocabulary

1 Match.

1 I'm writing
2 I'll delete
3 We can go
4 I visited
5 Billy usually surfs

a this message now that I've read it.
b an email to my cousin.
c the Internet for information.
d a new music website yesterday.
e online now and send this message.

2 Find six communication-related words. Then use these words to complete the sentences.

G	E	O	O	K	L	D	V	J	L	S	X
U	F	E	B	V	Q	C	A	D	L	O	U
O	R	M	D	O	H	H	B	G	O	C	S
D	O	W	N	L	O	A	D	M	X	I	K
A	S	D	T	E	X	T	I	N	G	A	J
C	O	N	N	E	C	T	I	O	N	L	S
C	T	Z	F	E	O	I	X	J	D	I	B
E	M	Z	U	X	T	N	H	A	O	S	Q
S	I	W	L	T	A	G	M	N	O	E	X
S	H	S	S	C	J	Y	J	Q	F	Y	C

1 I prefer emailing people or
____chatting____ with them online.

2 How much is an Internet
_____ for three months?

3 He works very long hours and he hasn't
got time to _____.

4 I want to _____ the *Arctic Monkeys* new song, but I don't know how.

5 She's been _____ all
morning – her fingers must hurt!

6 If you don't have Internet
_____, you can't go online.

3 Choose the correct answers.

1 affect
   a change as a result of something
   b create something new

2 face-to-face
   a when you are with another person and talking to them
   b when you email someone

3 log on
   a receive email messages
   b connect to a computer or website

4 hang out
   a spend time in a particular place or with particular people
   b think of something interesting

5 keep in touch
   a keep all the emails someone has sent you
   b write or talk to someone even though you do not see them often

Grammar

4 Complete the sentences.

1 'I'll send him an email,' said Kate.
Kate said that she _____would send_____ him an email.

2 'You can use my laptop,' said Beth.
Beth said that I _____ her laptop.

3 'My brother downloaded the film,' said Sara.
Sara said that her brother _____ the film.

4 'I must get an Internet connection,' said Paul.
Paul said that he _____ an Internet connection.

5 'I don't have a mobile phone,' said David.
David said that he _____ a mobile phone.

6 'I love surfing the Internet,' said Claire.
Claire said that she _____ the Internet.

5 Complete the sentences using reported speech.

1 'I'm deleting all my old messages.'
She said that she _was deleting all her old messages_.

2 'You must buy a better printer.'
He said that I _____.

3 'I use my laptop every day.'
She said that she _____.

4 'I received an email from Helen.'
He said that he _____.

5 'I've never visited that website.'
He said that he _____.

6 'We downloaded some new video clips.'
She said that they _____.

6 Read the dialogue and then complete the paragraph using reported speech.

Becky: (1) I want to download some good songs.
Grant: Cool. (2) There are lots of great songs to choose from.
Becky: (3) I'm looking for some that are really different.
Grant: (4) I like Bon Ivor's songs. (5) He has a new CD out.
Becky: You're right. (6) I heard his latest single on the radio yesterday!
Grant: Yes, (7) it's fantastic!
Becky: OK. (8) I'll download that one.
Grant: (9) You must log on to your computer and then (10) you can go to the Songs4All music site. It's the best for downloading songs and video clips.
Becky: Brilliant! Let's do it!

Becky said that she (1) _____wanted_____ to download some good songs. Grant told her that there (2) _____ lots of great songs to choose from. Becky said that she (3) _____ for some that were really different. Grant said that he (4) _____ Bon Ivor's songs and that he (5) _____ a new CD out. Becky said that she (6) _____ it on the radio, and Grant said that it (7) _____ fantastic. Becky said that she (8) _____ that one. Grant explained that she (9) _____ to her computer and that then she (10) _____ to the Songs4All music site.

Lesson 2

Vocabulary

1 Complete the crossword.

Across

2 They are going to _____ *select* _____ ten students for the science competition.

5 Can you believe that the _____ is over ten billion years old?

7 Are there _____ creatures on other planets?

Down

1 The spaceship will _____ the 'Red Planet' next month.

3 Does the staff _____ of more men or more women?

4 We need to _____ a meeting to talk about the new space programme.

6 Listen! I think they are sending us a _____ from outer space!

8 Do ghosts really _____?

Crossword grid:
- 1 Down: R
- 2 Across: S E L E C T
- 3 Down: C
- 4 Down: O
- 5 Across: U
- 6 Down: S
- 7 Across: I
- 8 Down: E

2 Choose the correct answers.

1 'Excuse me, Ms Warner. Could I ___ a phone call, please?'
'Yes, of course.'
a have
b make (circled)
c do

2 'Can I speak to Mr Shannon, please?'
'I'm afraid he's not here. Would you like to ___ a message?'
a leave
b put
c give

3 'Why don't you like Darren?'
'He ___ lies – that's why.'
a speaks
b says
c tells

4 'What's the matter?'
'I have to ___ a speech tomorrow, and I'm really nervous.'
a tell
b do
c make

5 'What are you two talking about?'
'We're ___ a conversation about aliens.'
a talking
b having
c doing

6 'What is that new teaching method they have ___?'
'Students use laptops instead of books.'
a developed
b received
c made

3 Complete the sentences with these words.

> across   back   off   on   up

1 Could you ask Mr James to call me _____ *back* _____ when he has a moment?

2 I believe he made _____ that story about seeing little green men in his garden.

3 Dad told me _____ for pulling the cat's tail.

4 I hope we managed to get the message _____ that there may be life on other planets.

5 I can't believe it! Joe just hung up _____ me!

Grammar

4 Complete the sentences using reported speech.

How old are you, Jane?

Ann asked Jane _how old she was_
_____.

Are you going to play basketball?

Pete asked his son _____
_____.

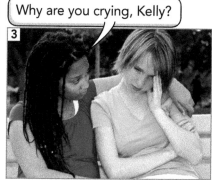

Why are you crying, Kelly?

Fiona asked her friend _____
_____.

Can you fix my printer, Michael?

Josh asked his cousin _____
_____.

Have you finished reading your book, Mum?

Sophia asked her mum _____
_____.

Did you do your homework, Steven?

Ellie asked her son _____
_____.

5 Look at the reported speech and write the direct speech.

1 He asked her where his MP3 player was.
   _Where is my MP3 player?_____

2 My father told me not to stay up late.
   _____

3 I asked if he could hear me.
   _____

4 He asked if I ever chatted online.
   _____

5 She asked where Tina had gone.
   _____

6 They asked me why I was leaving.
   _____

6 Circle the correct words.

1 The man asked me not speak / **to speak**.
2 She **asked** / said me to help her.
3 He asked **if** / have any signals had been received.
4 I **told** / said Tom not to shout so loudly.
5 He asked me to say / **tell** him where the planetarium was.
6 She said / **told** she wanted to buy a book about aliens.

11 Lesson 3

Vocabulary

1 Complete the sentences with these words.

> device   dictionary   order   portable   service   solution

1 Nobody has been able to find a _____solution_____ to this communication problem.
2 The food at the restaurant was quite good, but the _____ was awful.
3 This smartphone is an incredible _____.
4 The _____ says that 'aeropuerto' means 'airport' in Spanish.
5 If you _____ this web camera online, can you buy it cheaper?
6 They bought a _____ DVD player so they can watch films when they travel.

Grammar

2 Complete the sentences with reported speech.

1 'I'm meeting my sister at the Internet café today,' Amy said.
   Amy said that she _____was meeting_____ her sister at the Internet café _____that day_____.
2 'My father is giving a speech about modern communications tonight,' she said.
   She said that her father _____ a speech about modern communications
   _____.
3 'I'm going to try and talk to Mum this afternoon,' she said.
   She said that she _____ to try and talk to her mum _____.
4 'I phoned my friend Cindy yesterday, and she got the email too,' she said.
   She said that she _____ her friend Cindy _____, and that she
   _____ the email too.
5 'I chatted with my cousin on the Internet for four hours last week,' she said.
   She said that she _____ with her cousin on the Internet for four hours
   _____.

Express yourself!

3 **Read the sentences about what Elaine does. Then complete the sentences about William with so or neither and the correct form of the verb to show that the same things are also true for William.**

1 Elaine uses the Internet to keep in touch with friends.
   _____So does_____ William.
2 Elaine didn't buy an expensive mobile phone last week.
   _____ William.
3 Elaine is surfing the Internet at the moment.
   _____ William.
4 Elaine hasn't visited that website yet.
   _____ William.
5 Elaine can download photos.
   _____ William.

Writing

4 Read the article and circle the correct phrases.

What are the advantages and disadvantages of e-readers?

E-readers are cool little gadgets that are becoming more and more popular with both adults and children. This device is used to read books which have been downloaded from the Internet.

The **(1)** good thing about / on the other hand e-readers is that they are small and portable. They are very light, and you can take them with you almost anywhere. One of **(2)** the main advantages / what I like of e-readers is that they are environmentally friendly. Books are made from paper and paper comes from trees. With an e-reader, no trees need to be cut down so that you can enjoy your favourite book.

(3) Another drawback / On the other hand, many books are still not available for download. This means that you might not be able to use your e-reader to read the book of your choice. **(4)** The main problem / Another problem with e-readers is that they are expensive to buy, and book downloads can cost a lot too.

In my opinion, e-readers will never be as popular as books. It's true that they are easy to carry and kind to the environment. However, there is something wonderful about walking into a book shop and selecting that special book that you've been dying to read. It's also nice that most 'real' books are cheaper than the books you can download.

Remember!

We can use these phrases in an article to talk about advantages:
The good thing about … is that …
What I like about … is that …
One of the main advantages of … is that …
On the one hand, …

We can use these phrases in an article to talk about disadvantages:
On the other hand, …
The main problem with … is that …
Another drawback of … is …

5 Write an article with the title, 'What are the advantages and disadvantages of using smartphones?' Don't forget to use the phrases in the Remember! box. Use this plan to help you.

Paragraph 1
What are smartphones and who uses them? Why do they use them? How much/often do they use them?

Paragraph 2
Talk about the advantages of using a smartphone.
Advantage 1: …
Advantage 2: …

Paragraph 3
Talk about the disadvantages of using a smartphone.
Disadvantage 1: …
Disadvantage 2: …

Paragraph 4
What is your personal opinion?

Lesson 1

Vocabulary

1 Find seven shopping-related words. Then use these words to complete the sentences.

H	Z	W	P	U	B	A	R	G	A	I	N
F	A	S	H	I	O	N	A	B	L	E	F
J	S	C	U	Y	U	B	D	G	B	X	Y
M	A	R	K	E	T	C	E	B	F	H	K
L	L	Y	M	A	I	X	L	K	W	U	J
N	E	P	D	D	Q	O	I	Q	Y	M	S
B	S	D	Y	Z	U	E	V	A	Y	Y	M
T	Q	I	F	R	E	C	E	I	P	T	N
K	U	C	V	I	I	N	R	E	W	M	E
D	K	B	D	X	I	E	M	M	D	V	Q

1 In a floating _____market_____, goods are sold from boats.
2 If you order these jeans online, they will _____ them in three days.
3 You bought this dress for €12! Now that is a(n) _____!
4 I've just paid for these new jeans, but I didn't get a(n) _____. I'd better go back and get one.
5 I'm not going shopping this month. I'm going to wait for the _____ next month.
6 Short coats are very _____ at the moment.
7 That _____ sells clothes that I can't afford.

2 Complete the sentences with these words.

> antique   condition   department   designer
> issue   price

1 Have you ever heard of Harrods? It's one of the most expensive _____department_____ stores in London.
2 I'm selling my car. It's in perfect _____, so I should get lots of money for it.
3 You don't want to go in that shop! It only sells _____ clothes, and they're very expensive.
4 Have you read the January _____ of *National Geographic* magazine? It's got a few great articles in it.
5 Let's go into this _____ shop – I'm looking for an old clock for my collection.
6 Women's bags and shoes are half _____ today.

3 Choose the correct answers.

1 second-hand
   a something owned by someone else before you get it
   b something that is in good condition
2 order
   a ask for something to be brought to you
   b pay a high price for something
3 matching
   a having the same price
   b having the same colours, style or pattern
4 lens
   a part of a car that makes it go faster
   b part of a camera that light travels through
5 pad
   a something that gives you energy before you do a sport
   b something you wear on your body so you don't get hurt
6 collector
   a someone who collects things that are interesting or attractive
   b someone who owns an antique shop

82

Grammar

4 Complete the sentences with the causative using the words in brackets.

1 Craig ___had the shopping delivered___ (the shopping/deliver) yesterday.
2 She _____ (not/her photo/take) at the moment.
3 Next week, he _____ (the house/paint).
4 She _____ (her hair/do) once a week.
5 He _____ (can't/his car/fix) because he doesn't have enough money.
6 We _____ (invitations/print) last week.
7 I _____ (the pool/clean) tomorrow, I promise.

5 Write questions. Use the causative.

1 ? / you / your eyes / test / every year
___Do you have your eyes tested every year?___

2 ? / they / a swimming pool / build / next year
_____

3 ? / you / a new camera / deliver / yesterday evening
_____

4 ? / the children / their bedroom / paint / right now
_____

5 ? / she / the grass / cut / next week
_____

6 ? / he / often / his garden / clean up
_____

6 Choose the correct answers.

1 They ___ by a famous architect.
 a will have designed their house
 b will design their house
 c will have their house designed

2 She had the birthday cake ___ at the bakery.
 a made
 b make
 c making

3 Grandad ___ once a week.
 a the shopping delivers
 b has the shopping delivered
 c has delivered the shopping

4 Mr Jones ___ his glasses fixed today.
 a isn't having
 b hasn't
 c haven't

5 ___ a new gym built?
 a Will you
 b You will have
 c Will you have

6 She ___ by a professional photographer.
 a was taking her photo
 b had her photo taken
 c had taken her photo

Vocabulary

1 Match.

1	heels	☐ *d*	
2	refreshments	☐	
3	slippers	☐	
4	stall	☐	
5	flea market	☐	
6	material	☐	

2 Complete the sentences with these words.

baggy   formal   leather   scruffy   suit   tight

1 These shoes only cost €20 because they are not made of real _____leather_____. They're made of plastic.

2 This skirt is too _____. I need a bigger size.

3 Why are you wearing _____ clothes? I've never seen you in a suit and tie before.

4 Her new hairstyle doesn't really _____ her.

5 You can't go to your brother's wedding wearing this _____ old pair of jeans!

6 Tight trousers used to be in fashion, but _____ trousers are in fashion now.

3 Choose the correct answers.

1 Although this camera cost ___ €400, I still think it was a bargain.
   a up
   b above
   c over ←(circled)

2 As soon as they got to the flea market, they set ___ their stall.
   a out
   b up
   c in

3 When are you going to get rid ___ those awful ties, Dad?
   a for
   b of
   c off

4 Excuse me. Do you have this black and white shirt ___ my size?
   a in
   b on
   c of

5 These trainers are ___ special offer – I'm going to get them!
   a on
   b for
   c out

6 Although jeans have been around for years, they never go ___ of fashion.
   a up
   b in
   c out

Grammar

4 **Complete the sentences with** in order to **or** so that.

1 She's saving money ____in order to____ buy a pair of designer jeans.
2 Mum is going to buy some material _____ she can make me a new dress for the party.
3 I will take a taxi _____ I won't be late.
4 He wore a suit and tie _____ look good at the meeting.
5 Andy went into town _____ go shopping for a new laptop.
6 She gave me her email address _____ I could contact her.
7 I'll need your help _____ have everything ready for the party.

5 **Complete the second sentence so that it means the same as the first. Use the words in bold.**

1 These earrings are nice, but they're quite expensive.   **although**
____Although these earrings are____ nice, they're quite expensive.
2 It was snowing, but she wore a pair of heels.   **despite**
_____ it was snowing, she wore a pair of heels.
3 Although he didn't like the jacket very much, he decided to buy it.   **fact**
He decided to buy the jacket in _____ that he didn't like it.
4 I was really upset, but I didn't cry.   **spite**
In _____ I was really upset, I didn't cry.
5 She wore scruffy clothes even though she had a job interview.   **fact**
Despite _____ she had a job interview, she wore scruffy clothes.
6 They were tired, but they didn't go to bed.   **although**
_____, they didn't go to bed.

6 **Complete the paragraph with these words.**

although   although   despite   in order to   in spite   so that

Fur is one of the oldest known forms of clothing and has been worn by men and women throughout history. **(1)** ____Although____ it looks and feels fantastic, real fur is expensive and it's the result of horrific cruelty to animals. **(2)** _____ these things, people still walk around in fur coats and jackets. Are these people wearing animal fur **(3)** _____ of what animal lovers and conservationists might be saying about them? In most cases, the answer is no. They're wearing fake fur, a man-made material that looks like fur. Fake fur material was first made in the 1920s **(4)** _____ it could be used instead of real fur. Animal rights groups tried to get companies to advertise this new material **(5)** _____ stop the killing of animals like foxes, rabbits and bears. **(6)** _____ fake fur cannot match the characteristics of natural fur, it's cheaper, hand washable and comes in all sorts of different colours, from pale blue to dark purple.

12 Lesson 3

Vocabulary

1 Circle the correct words.

1 Helen will do / **find** any excuse to go shopping.
2 I wish you wouldn't save / spend all your money. You should think about your future.
3 Try not to get / go stressed about how you look.
4 That hat looks awful. Have / Do yourself a favour and get rid of it!
5 I'm not sensible / crazy about clothes, but I will buy things in the sales.
6 I love Internet shopping / centres because it saves me time and money.

Express yourself!

2 Look at the pictures and write the correct questions.

Can I help you?
How much is this?
What size do you take?
Where's the changing room?

Where's the changing room?

Speaking

3 Work with a partner. Imagine you're in one of these shops. Use the information and the phrases from Express yourself! to make a dialogue.

Clothes shop	Sports shop	Shoe shop
T-shirt	skateboard	slippers
jeans	skis	heels
jacket	tennis racket	walking boots

Good morning. Can I help you?

Yes, I want to buy a jacket.

Writing

4 Read the report and choose the most suitable headings for the paragraphs. There are two headings you don't need.

Advantages Aim Conclusion Drawbacks Internet companies
Local computer shops Shopping online and shopping in stores

Online shopping: Is it always a good thing?

(1) _Aim_

The purpose of this report is to discuss whether using the Internet is a good way to do your shopping.

(2) _____

Until quite recently people did not have a choice about where to shop. Most shopping was done in shops and stores. Shopping online grew popular in the past few years. The first online shops opened in the 1990s.

(3) _____

Shopping online is very easy – all you need is a computer and a credit card. There are many sites you can visit, and there is a huge variety of items to choose from. In addition, when you shop online, you do it while sitting comfortably at home. This means that you do not have to go out when the weather is bad.

(4) _____

However, when you shop online, you can't actually see what you're buying – you can only see a photo of it. When it gets delivered, you may realise that it was not quite what you wanted. This is especially true for clothes. Shopping online can also be dangerous because your credit card information may get stolen.

(5) _____

Although online shopping is easy and offers a great choice of products, it has some serious drawbacks. You should think carefully before you order anything from a website because you may not be happy with the results.

Remember!

A report includes several paragraphs, each of which has got a heading. In the first paragraph you should state the aim of the report, and in the last paragraph you should give a conclusion.

5 Write a report with the title, 'Shopping during sales: Is it a good idea?' Give each of your paragraphs a heading. Use this plan to help you. Add notes of your own to the plan.

Aim
Briefly describe the purpose of the report.

Paragraph 1: Description
How often do shops in your area have sales? What items can you buy during sales? Do all shops in your area have sales?

Paragraph 2: Advantages
Talk about the advantages of shopping during sales.
Advantage 1: …
Advantage 2: …

Paragraph 3: Drawbacks
Talk about the drawbacks of shopping during sales.
Drawback 1: …
Drawback 2: …

Conclusion
Give your conclusion in favour of or against shopping during sales.

Reading

1 Read the text about a special kind of market.

Souks, open-air marketplaces, have existed since ancient times. In the past, souks used to be outside big cities, in places where caravans would stop and people would display goods for sale. At that time, souks were more than a market to buy and sell goods. They were festivals with dancing, storytelling, poetry competitions and snake charmers.

The way these markets are organised might be a little different today, but they are still a great place to buy a variety of items from food and clothes to pets. Although each neighbourhood within a city may have a local souk selling food and other essentials, the main souk is usually a central marketplace, where jewellery, spices, wooden sculptures and other goods are sold.

In some places there are weekly markets that are named from the day of the week when they are held. For example, the Wednesday Market in Amman sells second-hand goods, and the Friday Market in Baghdad specialises in pets.

If you have the chance to visit a souk, you should certainly do so. You can enjoy the local culture, browse around the stalls, pick up souvenirs but also have fun bargaining for a better price!

2 Write T (true) or F (false).

1 In the past, souks were inside big cities.   F
2 Souks used to offer entertainment for shoppers. ☐
3 There is always one souk in the same city. ☐
4 Souks don't only sell food. ☐
5 The Friday Market in Baghdad specialises in second-hand goods. ☐
6 In souks, you always pay the price written on the goods. ☐

Vocabulary

3 Choose the correct answers.

1 The man at the shop said that an Internet ___ wasn't expensive.
   a signal
   (b) connection
   c access

2 It's time we ___ rid of all those old clothes.
   a took
   b made
   c got

3 I bought this dress in the ___. It was half price.
   a sales
   b bargains
   c refunds

4 Martha is moving to Australia, but she promised she would ___ in touch.
   a reach
   b select
   c keep

5 Most kids said that they spent a lot of their free time ___ their friends.
   a texting
   b chatting
   c socialising

6 'Why are you so stressed?'
   'I have to ___ a speech tonight and I don't like talking in front of a lot of people.'
   a tell
   b leave
   c make

7 She said that it had taken her more than an hour to ___ the film from the Internet.
   a download
   b browse
   c surf

8 Can life ___ on another planet in our galaxy?
   a select
   b develop
   c reach

9 I had a new TV ___ to my house yesterday.
   a ordered
   b delivered
   c held

10 I can't stand skinny jeans! I hope they go out ___ fashion.
   a for
   b over
   c of

11 ___ will be served during the break and after the show.
   a Refreshments
   b Items
   c Varieties

12 I asked him for an explanation but he just ___ on me.
   a called back
   b hung up
   c told off

Grammar

4 Choose the correct answers.

1 I asked my dad ___ so fast.
   a to not drive
   (b) not to drive
   c not drive

2 He ___ he would be late.
   a tell me
   b told
   c told me

3 She asked me if I ___ made for the wedding.
   a was having a new dress
   b have a new dress
   c was a new dress having

4 They said they ___ me a new mobile phone.
   a would buy
   b will have bought
   c did buy

5 Zoe said that she had bought the CD the day ___.
   a next
   b ago
   c before

6 Dan emailed me and asked what ___ that afternoon.
   a I was doing
   b was I doing
   c I am doing

7 She told me not to speak at ___ moment.
   a this
   b that
   c those

8 ___ your shopping delivered to the house?
   a Do you have
   b Are they
   c Have they

9 ___ his scruffy appearance, he got the job!
   a Despite
   b In spite
   c Although

10 In spite of ___ very rich, he drives an old car.
   a to be
   b being
   c be

11 She wore her new shoes to work ___ to look fashionable.
   a for
   b in order
   c so

12 Although ___ those designer jeans, I can't afford them.
   a liking
   b I will like
   c I like

89

Crossword puzzles

Units 1–2

Complete the crossword puzzle.

Across

6 The first telescope was created by the famous Italian _____*astronomer*_____, Galileo Galilei.

9 There was a _____ sunset last night.

Down

1 The Statue of Liberty is the most famous _____ of New York.

2 _____, I didn't have my camera with me, or I would have taken a photo of it.

3 He works for a _____ that produces electrical goods.

4 A _____ is an area where there's little rain and not many plants.

5 The _____ of Olympian Zeus in Athens was built in the 6th century BC.

7 We followed the _____ until we came to a gate.

8 A _____ is a place where water naturally flows out from the ground.

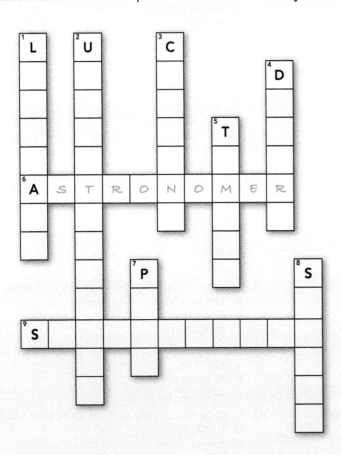

Units 3 – 4

Complete the crossword puzzle.

Across

3   This is when you carry goods or people from one place to another in a bus, coach, etc.
5   This is an event which causes great harm, damage or death.
7   This is when a particular animal or plant stops existing.
8   This is a small flying insect that bites people and animals.
10 This is the natural environment in which an animal or plant usually lives.

Down

1   This describes someone who can wait calmly for a long time.
2   This describes someone who does careless things without thinking.
4   This is the foot of an animal that has claws or nails.
6   This is a forest in a tropical area where it rains a lot.
9   These are small flat pieces that cover the skin of snakes, fish, etc.

Crossword puzzles

Units 5 – 6

Complete the crossword puzzle.

Across

2 If the new shopping centre opens, a lot of the _____Local_____ shops will close.

4 Mark and his brother were two of the ten _____ of the plane crash.

8 The famous inventor Benjamin Franklin worked as a printer _____ for his older brother.

10 This is a _____ that Vincent van Gogh painted of himself.

Down

1 He's got a _____ in history from Oxford.

3 Do you think a _____ could repair Grandad's broken armchair?

5 A helicopter picked up the _____ soldiers and took them to the hospital.

6 _____ is usually a happy time for most people.

7 A _____ of fifty people looks after the 400 passengers during the cruise.

9 Our bathroom has flooded – we need to call a _____.

Units 7 – 8

Complete the crossword puzzle.

Across

2 These are the words of a song.
3 This describes someone who is very thin.
6 This is another word for football.
8 This is when you show or describe how to do something.

Down

1 This is how you feel when you are very tired.
2 This is a picture of the countryside.
4 This is when you feel nervous and worried.
5 This is a person who writes music, especially classical music.
7 This is writing or drawings on walls, doors, etc in public places.

Crossword puzzles

Units 9 – 10

Complete the crossword puzzle.

Across

4 ___Paragliding___ is the sport of jumping out of a plane with a special parachute.

6 Was her death an accident or did her husband _____ her?

9 She was sent to prison for a crime that she didn't _____.

10 An _____ is someone who tries to find out the truth about a crime, accident, etc.

Down

1 The _____ of YouTube were three employees of an Internet company.

2 Is the castle really _____ by the spirit of its dead owner?

3 Why don't you put on your _____ and mask and go snorkelling?

5 He likes trying exciting and often dangerous things – he's very _____.

7 The security guard described the bank _____ to the police officers.

8 A _____ baseball bat is one metre long.

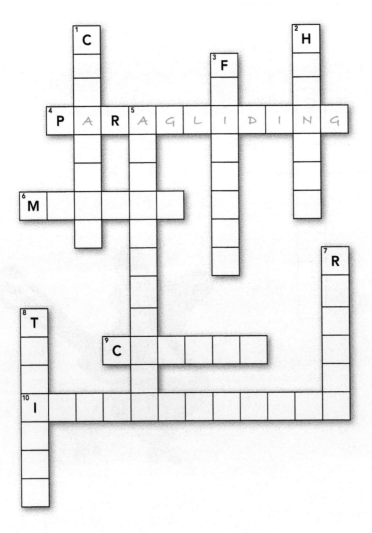

Units 11 – 12

Complete the crossword puzzle.

Across

1 This is a set of questions that you ask a large number of people to find out their opinions about something.
6 This is when you send someone a written message on a mobile phone.
7 This is when you take part in a discussion with someone on the Internet.
8 This is a collection of things that are all different from one another.
9 This describes something that is popular at a particular time.

Down

1 This is when you carefully choose something as being the best or the most suitable.
2 This is something that you buy cheaply or for less than its usual price.
3 This is when you take goods to people's houses or places of work.
4 This is when you look at goods in a shop, but you're not sure if you want to buy anything.
5 This is a piece of paper that you are given and shows that you've paid for something.